DWELL

SANDRA BYRD

DWELL

90 DAYS AT HOME WITH GOD

Our Daily Bread
Publishing®

These devotions were previously published in *The One Year Home and Garden Devotions* (Tyndale 2015).

Requests for permission to quote from this book should be directed to: Permissions Department, Our Daily Bread Publishing, PO Box 3566, Grand Rapids, MI 49501, or contact us by email at permissionsdept@odb.org.

Scripture quotations, unless otherwise indicated, are taken from the Holy Bible, New International Version®, NIV®. Copyright © 1973, 1978, 1984, 2011 by Biblica, Inc.™ Used by permission of Zondervan. All rights reserved worldwide. www.zondervan.com.

Scripture quotations marked esv are taken from the ESV® Bible (The Holy Bible, English Standard Version®), copyright © 2001 by Crossway, a publishing ministry of Good News Publishers. Used by permission. All rights reserved.

Scripture quotations marked msg are taken from *The Message*, copyright © 1993, 2002, 2018 by Eugene H. Peterson. Used by permission of NavPress, represented by Tyndale House Publishers. All rights reserved.

Scripture quotations marked nlt are taken from the Holy Bible, New Living Translation, copyright © 1996, 2004, 2015 by Tyndale House Foundation. Used by permission of Tyndale House Publishers, Inc., Carol Stream, Illinois 60188. All rights reserved.

Scripture quotations marked voice are from The Voice™. Copyright © 2012 by Ecclesia Bible Society. Used by permission. All rights reserved.

Interior design by Jody Langley
Photo credits on p. 128

ISBN: 978-1-64070-227-1

Printed in the United States of America
23 24 25 26 27 28 29 30 / 9 8 7 6 5 4 3 2

For my beloved daughter, Elizabeth,
who created a beautiful home in which to
dwell with her family and her God.

Introduction

Home. It's where we long to return at the end of the day or a season away, the place we honestly share ourselves with those who know and love us best. We attach the word *home* to many emotionally resonant phrases: childhood home, Grandma's house, Mom's house, dream home, forever home. Home might be where you live now, where you grew up, or the place where you find your beloveds. We meet colleagues at a restaurant, but we invite friends into our home for a meal specially prepared with them in mind to express love and intimacy. No matter where the Lord plants us in the world, He wants us to settle in and make a home (Jeremiah 29:5).

God made it clear from the start that He desires to be intimate with us wherever we dwell. With God, at home together works both ways: He is our home, and He makes His home within us. He dwells in us (Ephesians 3:17; Hebrews 3:6), and we dwell in Him (1 John 4:13). It's as tightly knit as can be.

In Numbers 28, the Lord reminded the Israelites about the food offerings He expected them to present. Sometimes those food offering passages in the Old Testament can be confusing, but this one becomes clear as you read the chapter. The Lord asked for those offerings to be presented to Him each morning and every twilight—when His family ate. He asked them to offer the same kinds of foods they were serving to themselves. He wanted to sit down with His family and enjoy an intimate meal.

John affirms that Jesus made His dwelling among us (John 1:14). When Jesus came to earth, He continued to show us that He wanted to share intimacy with His people through shared meals. He ate roasted fish with His disciples. He dined with tax collectors. He shared the Last

7

Supper with His closest friends, a meal we continue to celebrate with and for Him. He tells us that if we love Him, we will obey Him, and when we obey Him, the Father will love us, and He will come and make a home with us (John 14:23).

I say in jest that I have offered many burnt offerings to my family members over the years. Still, all kidding aside, it's important to me to ask the Lord, the provider of everything that ever appears in my home and on my table, to join us in my dwelling and have the place of honor at the feast. He's my most welcome, most honored family member, and I'll make the extra effort to ensure He's never overlooked and always feels comfortable in my house and at my table.

God continues to open my eyes to see His presence in my home and garden, and He teaches me through them and grows close to me through that leading and presence. I originally wrote *The One Year Home and Garden Devotions* filled with those insights. Here, I have curated from that book the ninety pieces that best show how to be at home with God and how He displays His love and companionship with us right where we live. I've fortified the Scripture verses and enhanced some of the works to make them even more resonant for you, cherished reader.

When I say I'm at home with someone, I feel secure and filled with peace. I laugh and I learn. I hope these devotions, day by day, will lead you to a place where no matter where you dwell, you always feel at home with God.

If you say, "The Lord is my refuge,"
and you make the Most High your dwelling,
no harm will overtake you.

PSALM 91:9–10

Draw Near to God

One of my favorite things is to sit on the couch with people and pets that I love—in every season. Autumn finds me there with squishy throw pillows and warm blankets; winter brings a fire in the fireplace. I look out the window from that couch and watch the world wake up and warm up during the spring and summer. But even though our couch is well worn, I don't want to replace it because it allows me to sink into coziness in all the right places.

If my husband is home, we sit on it together and read or watch TV, cuddling sometimes. When my daughter comes to visit, we lean against each other and watch movies. My son and I read side by side, and my friends and I sit close enough to share prayers and coffee. If I'm the only one home, I simply have to pat the couch a few times, and my dog jumps up and *sitsthisclose* to my leg. She comes near.

The Lord has told us that He wants to be close to us (1 John 4:19); He paid the ultimate price to make that closeness happen. People have often asked, if God wants to get close to us, why does the verse say we must come close to Him, and then He will come close to us (James 4:8)? Why not the other way around? But here's the deal: He has already made the first move by making a way to cover sin and create intimacy (Hebrews 10:22). It's as if He is saying, "I cleared the space on the couch. Your move next—want to come over?" And then when we do, we feel Him and His presence.

God has made a space for you. Scoot a little closer.

Come near to God and he will come near to you.
JAMES 4:8

Paradise from My Upstairs Window

One afternoon I ran around madly, trying to finish the chores before company arrived. The last task was to strip and remake the bed in the guest room. As I did that, I took a moment to stop and look out the window right across from the bed.

It was a rare clear day, not a puff of a cloud in the sky, and off in the distance sat Mount Rainier. Everyone around here simply calls it The Mountain, not just because its near relative, Mount St. Helens, lost her head a few years back and is now much harder to see. No, it's called The Mountain because it's the tallest and most majestic. For those who enjoy a relaxing walk and hike, the best part of Mount Rainier is called Paradise.

Paradise is often dotted with purple and red alpine flowers, bathed in sunlight, and soothed by cool breezes. To walk its gentle slope is to preview heaven. I don't get to visit Paradise often, but I catch a glimpse of it from my home nearly every week.

The Lord has told us that this world is not our home (Hebrews 13:14). Although there are many wonderful things here, and God desires for us to be filled with peace and joy in our present lives (Romans 15:13), something much better lies ahead for those who believe. The Bible offers a few clues as to what heaven will be like (Revelation 21), but Jesus promised that it's a place He prepared for us (John 14:2–3), where He'll be with us, and where we'll be with our brothers and sisters in the faith throughout eternity.

In my day-to-day life, when I listen to a baby's laughter, when I receive the gift of a hug or a card in the mail from a friend, when I share a meal with new friends or worship with old ones, I catch a little glimpse of paradise from my earthbound window. When do you glimpse paradise?

> He said, "Jesus, remember me when you
> come into your kingdom."
> Jesus answered him, "Truly I tell you,
> today you will be with me in paradise."
> LUKE 23:42–43

Running Away from Home

Well, we have all wanted to run away from home at one time or another, haven't we? When did you last have that impulse? As a child? Or maybe it was only last week!

I remember the first time I wanted to run away from home; I was about six years old. I took a brown paper grocery sack into my bedroom, filled it with a few clothes, books, and toys, and then topped it off with my precious, beloved Mrs. Beasley doll. I went into the living room and then opened the front door to find it raining out. I didn't want to walk down the street in the rain, and where would I go, anyway? So, instead, I stood wedged between the screen and the door long enough, I hoped, to make everyone worried and then came back into the house. I don't remember making a grand announcement, and I probably just quietly unpacked my brown sack and settled my doll back on the bed.

Even now, as an adult, there are times when I want to run away from home. I feel overwhelmed by my circumstances. I don't see a good solution no matter how many options I consider. Things have not turned out as expected or hoped, and I feel real despair drilling into my soul. I'm angry with God. Didn't He say the faithful prayers of a righteous person would avail much (James 5:16)? Was I not righteous? Faithful? What had gone wrong?

Then when I stop between the door and the screen and look at my rainy options without God, I think, *Where would I even go* (Psalm 139:7)? I don't *want* to go; I just feel defeated. I open the door and walk back toward Him, and He helps me unpack my bag and holds me for a while, and I feel soothed and cared for. I don't always know right then how things will work out. But He's there with me, cherishing me. He is my home, and I will not run away from Him.

I am always with you;
you hold me by my right hand.
You guide me with your counsel,
and afterward you will take me into glory.
Whom have I in heaven but you?

PSALM 73:23-25

Good Excuses

A while back, some friends came over for dinner. Because we all lead busy lives and they live hours away, we don't get to see them very often. So we sat around the fire pit long into the night, looking for good excuses for them to remain with us. More coffee, more dessert, another important conversation, anything. We wanted to give them a reason to tarry . . . to stay, to abide with us a while longer.

A few months later, it was time for our son to return to his apartment after a holiday with us. Although we didn't want him to drive while tired, I wished he would stay a little longer—for one more meal, even one more hour. I wanted a good reason for him to tarry, stay with us, and abide.

To abide means to remain together, linger in love, and be comfortably entwined, twisted together gently like ivy and oak or like the branches of wisteria. Scripture tells us, "Whoever loves his brother abides in the light, and in him there is no cause for stumbling" (1 John 2:10 ESV). It's easy not to stumble when the light is on—you can see where you're going. Loving our brothers and sisters, our fellow believers, is a sign that we are remaining in the light of Christ. In 1 Corinthians, Paul tells us, "Faith, hope, and love abide, these three; but the greatest of these is love" (1 Corinthians 13:13 ESV). It's a gentle, pleasant thought to imagine faith, hope, and love tarrying at my home, lingering in and after my conversations, pressing in for one more hour, like trusted, beloved friends.

I wish to abide with my friends, and Jesus calls us His friends (John 15:13–15). He lingers among us. I'm honored that He chooses to abide with me; I must continue to choose to abide with and in Him.

Abide in me, and I in you. As the branch
cannot bear fruit by itself, unless it abides
in the vine, neither can you, unless you
abide in me.

JOHN 15:4 ESV

DAY 5
Ripe and Ripening

My daughter has a cascade of thorny blackberry bushes growing behind her house, and I love to sit out there with her, picking them together and then eating them together. The bushes are on my daughter's private property, so we get the whole haul to ourselves. We head out with little cups, and each of us pop one berry into the container and one into the mouth! The hardest part, though, is waiting till the fruit is ripe.

For some reason, the berries do not ripen all at the same time but rather over the course of several months. You can find a luscious, dark berry that pops with sweetness growing alongside a slightly lighter berry that has a blend of tang and sugar. Everyone knows not to pluck the red berries unless they want an hour-long pucker and maybe a sick stomach. That fruit is not bad; it's simply not ripe.

In our lives, too, we have potential that has not yet had time to ripen (Philippians 3:12–14). So often, we look toward the red berries on our branches, embarrassed that we are not further along in our faith or ashamed that we have made mistakes. But we are works in progress; God is working on and in us (Philippians 2:13). Someday our red berries will darken to black; they will be sweet and lovely and ready to be harvested for the good of God's Kingdom.

Be patient and loving with yourself. You were created to bear fruit over time, which means that you'll always have some red berries waiting to ripen, and that's okay.

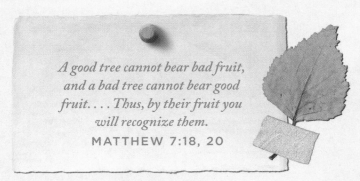

A good tree cannot bear bad fruit, and a bad tree cannot bear good fruit.... Thus, by their fruit you will recognize them.
MATTHEW 7:18, 20

DAY 6
Leftovers

Have you ever bitten into an apple or eaten most of the way through it, only to discover a worm at the center? It will kill your appetite for a few days. A friend of mine bought a prepared salad and found a dead bug at the bottom after eating most of it. As a result, salad was off her menu for some time.

When God led the Israelites out of Egypt and into the desert, He provided food daily. The food was called manna, which He provided through miraculous means. By description, it was sweet, savory, and crispy, so it covered a lot of taste preferences (Exodus 16:31; Numbers 11:7–8). God instructed Moses that the people were not to save manna from one day to the next, except for the Sabbath. Some of them ignored the instructions, though, and when they went to eat their hoarded manna, they found it loaded with maggots. Ick!

God tells us in the New Testament to ask for our daily bread (Matthew 6:11)—not our weekly bread or our monthly bread—instead, to trust Him to provide what we need day by day. Hoarding resources shows a lack of trust that what we need next Wednesday will be there—maybe not by Tuesday night, but by Wednesday. And as we shall not live by bread alone (Matthew 4:4), I think I'm to spend time in the Word day by day, too. The word of encouragement I needed last week is likely not the instruction I'll need next, but the right word in the right season is guaranteed to be there!

Moses said to them, "It is the bread the LORD has given you to eat.
This is what the LORD has commanded:
'Everyone is to gather as much as they need. . . .'"
Then Moses said to them, "No one is to keep any of it until morning."
However, some of them paid no attention to Moses; they kept part of
it until morning, but it was full of maggots and began to smell.
EXODUS 16:15-16, 19-20

Topiaries

Because I love all things French, I desperately wanted to have a topiary—a plant clipped or trained into a deliberate shape—inside my house. I had some pretty silk ones, but I wanted to try growing a live one.

There are many plants you can use for topiary—some are small trees or shrubs and some have long, winding shoots. If you choose a vine or ivy, you must plant it in the pot when it's small and young. After that, you nestle in the frame. Choosing the frame is perhaps the most fun part of doing topiary. I saw all kinds of classic frames—a ball, two balls, a cone, a tower—and some fun ones—a chicken, a dachshund, a Loch Ness monster. I settled on one that looked like the Eiffel Tower and placed it into my pot.

Over the months, as the plant grew, I would take its long, leafy tendrils and weave them through the iron frame. The shoots would grow longer; I'd incorporate them further. With sunlight, water, and plant food, I managed to grow a work of art. My topiary was the exact shape of the frame inside it, even though the frame could no longer be seen.

What kind of framework am I growing around? To whom do I shape my life (Romans 12:2)? And can I do that and remain . . . me? There are many potential frames we can choose from—though I'm guessing none of us want to look like the Loch Ness monster—but choose we must. The beauty for Christians is that we can be both delightfully different, unique, with a style all our own, and still, to others, look like Christ (2 Corinthians 3:18).

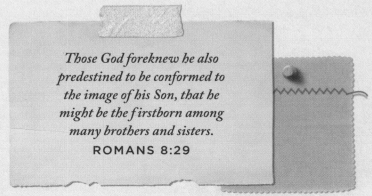

Those God foreknew he also predestined to be conformed to the image of his Son, that he might be the firstborn among many brothers and sisters.

ROMANS 8:29

Polished and Perfect

One rainy day while I was doing a New Year's cleaning out of the garage, I happened upon a stash of toys I'd saved from my kids' childhoods. One favorite—the rock tumbler—beckoned. It was a favorite not only because we'd had fun together fashioning agate key chains and quartz rings but because I, too, had cherished a rock tumbler in my childhood.

I reached for it, and as I held it in my hands, I recalled the week we'd purchased it as a treat—and a distraction. We'd just learned that our children would have to leave the school they enjoyed, one where they felt safe and I thought they were in a protected environment. Instead, financial pressures caused us to make some hard choices, and the school had to go. *It's not fair*, I told God. *They are safe there.*

But maybe He didn't want my children to be safe necessarily; instead, He wanted them to be useful, satisfied, and fulfilled. Christlike. I'd looked down at our rock tumbler. We'd throw a bunch of sharp-edged, broken stones into it with some grit and water, then start the motor. The action of those sharp stones bumping up against one another would produce the smooth, refined gems we desired (Philippians 3:21). Till the rocks had been tumbled and scraped, they were rough and common.

Likewise, the Lord wanted my children to be the polished, beautiful, and useful gems He and I both knew they could be. However, that wouldn't come about without bumping up against some sharp circumstances. I am thankful that a trusted hand turned and guided the tumbler that would transform my kids into just who God wanted them to be.

> *Dear brothers and sisters, when troubles of any*
> *kind come your way, consider it an opportunity for*
> *great joy. For you know that when your faith is*
> *tested, your endurance has a chance to grow. So let*
> *it grow, for when your endurance is fully developed,*
> *you will be perfect and complete, needing nothing.*
> JAMES 1:2-4 NLT

Welcome Brownies

I scrolled through the list of houses online, page by page, looking for the one that might be my family's next home. Among the callouts of kitchen upgrades and lovely views, a single line on a listing caught my eye and made me stop clicking ahead.

"One of the neighbors is known to deliver homemade brownies."

It seemed quaint, somehow, a memory of a bygone welcome-wagon era. A neighbor who did not wait in an idling car, windows up, till he could pull in the garage and close the door behind him. Someone who baked with a purpose, to feed and treat not only his own family but those he shared a street with, and in some respects, a life. The listing mentioned it pointed to the fact that it was recognized as both unusual and desirable.

"Maybe this is the one," I said to my husband.

"Because of the brownies?"

I nodded.

We did indeed buy that house, and the neighbor came over with flowers one week and brownies a month later. Another neighbor shared fresh cherry tomatoes from the bounty of her greenhouse. I reciprocated with jam the following summer.

We hear a lot about *random* acts of kindness—buying coffee for the person in the car behind you, for example. Not spoken of as frequently, but perhaps even more important, are *deliberate* acts of kindness (Philippians 3:3–4). When we choose people to be the focus of our good intentions, sharing our bounty, thinking of them ahead of ourselves, it speaks to them of how we value them. For those of us in the house of God, it shares insight into our true home.

> *Let your light shine before others, that they*
> *may see your good deeds and glorify your*
> *Father in heaven.*
> MATTHEW 5:16

Dormant

Every year, come September, I finish watering and feeding my plants. After that, the rain takes care of the maintenance watering, and the plants shouldn't need to eat again till they start a new growth period in early spring. Autumn and winter are periods of dormancy for garden plants. They don't grow taller, fuller, or develop leaves or blossoms. Instead, using what energy they do have, they push their roots deeper and wider. Or sleep.

Dormancy is a tough season for plants. The weather is colder and windier, and they have less protection. There is little sun to bless their branches and lots of ice to curse them. It's when they put their heads down and bear things out.

When spring arrives, at last, the plants begin to let loose. I watch them leaf out, each in its season, and pop out tiny buds ready to blossom. Last year's perennials grow another several inches, or maybe even a foot if the plant is a fast grower. This is the time to feed them again.

We, too, have periods of dormancy in life. We've got our heads down and our teeth clenched, and we are doing what we can to get through a cold, icy season. But all the time, whether we realize it or not, our roots are growing stronger against the whipping wind (Colossians 2:6–7), our branches are growing tougher bark against that ice. When it comes time for us to blossom again, when the sun shines once more, we'll be ready to face the new season in beautiful grandeur (Psalm 1:3).

Is this a cold season for you? Hold on. Sunshine is on the way.

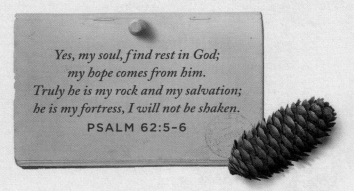

Yes, my soul, find rest in God;
my hope comes from him.
Truly he is my rock and my salvation;
he is my fortress, I will not be shaken.

PSALM 62:5-6

Sowing and Weeping

Without rain, nothing grows. Instead, plants dry out, wither, and blow away. I don't often see this lesson play out in the Pacific Northwest, known for its rain, but one year was particularly dry. Even sprinklers, tossing hose-fed drops hither and yon, could not provide the deep soaking required for real growth. Many young landscapes perished, but my husband and I still planted a few favorite plants in faith and with care.

Our young family was also undergoing a trying season that year, and the drought seemed an apt metaphor. Things were going wrong on many fronts, and as most people know, fighting a battle on more than one front leads to exhaustion and the potential for failure. Eventually, brought to our knees, we spent the next few months praying and crying, praying and crying (1 Peter 5:6–7). At long last came the rain.

The rain of our tears watered the seeds sown during that season: seeds of faith, perseverance, and hope despite discouraging odds and wondering without wandering. God restored our fortunes in ways we could not have dreamed of (1 Peter 5:10); He filled us with joy. Nothing would have grown if we had not planted the seeds before the rains came. Likewise, nothing would have grown if there were seeds but no rain to water them. But both—seeds and rain, working together—brought sheaves of blessing in good season.

Hold on; joy is coming. Do not be afraid to let the tears fall, but sow good seeds, too.

The LORD has done great things for us,
and we are filled with joy. . . .
Those who sow with tears
will reap with songs of joy.
Those who go out weeping,
carrying seed to sow,
will return with songs of joy,
carrying sheaves with them.
PSALM 126:3, 5-6

Pruned

We have two giant Chocolate Cherry tomato plants in our backyard. They are like babies to my husband. He checks them first thing in the morning and counts blossoms and fruit after work. He sprays them with organic spray and stakes them where they need it.

For a month, the bushes grew so large that they spilled over their cages onto the landscape stones, crowding the rest of the garden. There were many branches and leaves on each plant. As the summer wore on, though, it was clear that some branches were loaded with fruit, but some had no fruit at all.

The fruitless branches were plenty green, to be sure. But because they were not bearing, they were hoarding resources that the fruit-bearing branches needed for the green tomatoes to mature to red. And the big leaves of the fruitless branches were blocking the sun from other productive branches.

"They have to go," my husband said. I agreed.

With a sharp trimmer, he cut back enough branches to completely fill our yard-waste container, shaping and snipping with great care (John 15:2). When he was finished, what was left were the fruit-bearing branches, those with promising yellow blossoms and those with budding fruit. If we had kept the nonproductive branches, the productive branches would continue to be robbed of the resources they needed to ripen the fruit. One doesn't grow a tomato plant, after all, for beautiful foliage. One grows it for fruit, and the conscientious gardener prunes with that in mind. Our Master Gardener can be trusted to know what and where to cut to bring forth the very best fruit (Galatians 5:22–23).

> *I am the vine; you are the branches.*
> *If you remain in me and I in you,*
> *you will bear much fruit; apart from*
> *me you can do nothing.*
> JOHN 15:5

Lessons from Squirrels

One week a huge storm blew into my town. The electricity flickered on and off, and the howling wind brought to mind all the unfriendly things that could be outside. Then suddenly, the lights snapped off for good, and a terrible cracking noise stopped us in our tracks. We stood absolutely still before running to the window to see what had happened.

A huge tree had cracked and fallen, just missing our house. We thanked God for keeping us safe . . . but what about our chubby animal family that had been squirreling away nuts in their home in that tree?

The next day we stepped out onto the patio to see what had happened. The largest tree in our backyard had broken nearly in half. All that was left was a jagged, sharp-edged stump. The rest of the tree had thudded into our yard and spilled over into our neighbors' yard. The squirrels, who had been faithfully storing nuts in that tree in preparation for winter, looked as confused as we did.

Why that tree? they seemed to ask. *It seemed so strong. We never expected this to happen.* But then we watched as they began carting their stash of nuts out of that tree and into another one standing firmly nearby. They were busily starting over in an even stronger tree trunk—one that had many more warm fir branches and had proved its superior strength by surviving the storm.

Life is often worrisome and dangerous. The "tree" we don't expect to fall does, and we scratch our heads and wonder why. But soon, we see that the roof wasn't hit and everyone is safe. While the circumstance may not be what we planned for, and we may not even understand what happened or why, with God's ever-present help (Psalm 46:1), we move forward with a new plan and stash our acorns somewhere stronger and even better.

If you say, "The LORD is my refuge,"
and you make the Most High your dwelling,
no harm will overtake you.
PSALM 91:9–10

DAY 14
Squirreling Things Away

I love the phrase "squirreling things away" because it's so wonderfully evocative; anyone who has watched a squirrel scamper to a hidden nest or hollow tree, cheeks heavy with acorns, knows just what it means.

Some people don't squirrel anything away (Proverbs 21:20). They eat their acorns as soon as they get them and then have nothing left to get them through the cold, wet, and windy winter. On the other hand, some people squirrel *everything* away for a rainy day that never comes. By faith, we are led to a happy medium between these two extremes. Hoarders come to understand that acorns buried and forgotten can rot and be of no use (Luke 12:18–19). Spendthrifts come to realize that while the Lord will provide pleasure and joys today and tomorrow, we must save a little for rainy days (Proverbs 13:16).

I love to look out my kitchen window and watch squirrels working together. One finds, another brings back to the nest. They are partners, each doing his share. I think we're to be like those squirrels. From what I have, I save some and share some. And you do the same. Jesus tells us we will be known by our love for one another, and James says our faith is proven by our deeds. When we have faith that the Lord will provide tomorrow as He does today, we needn't stuff our cheeks. We needn't party like there's no tomorrow when we have faith that He will bring joy tomorrow as He does today.

Do not worry, saying, "What shall we eat?" or
"What shall we drink?" or "What shall we wear?"
For the pagans run after all these things, and
your heavenly Father knows that you need them.
But seek first his kingdom and his righteousness,
and all these things will be given to you as well.
Therefore do not worry about tomorrow,
for tomorrow will worry about itself.
Each day has enough trouble of its own.

MATTHEW 6:31–34

27

Planting Ahead

So by now, you know I love squirrels! One autumn day, I looked out my window at the landscape turning brown and dry with the season, and I spied a squirrel running off with a bulb, newly dug up (and probably recently planted!), twice the size of his mouth. Would he eat it on the spot, store it in the ground and eat it later, or perhaps bury and forget it?

Next spring, I had an answer. To one side of the front door, I had a lovely display of neatly arranged bulbs—crocus and daffodil, and tulip in a steady procession. To the other, a few yards away, a crazy quilt of colors and flowers grew where bulbs had been removed, reburied, and forgotten. I have to say, knowing the story behind that pretty patch and its unexpected splendor, I enjoyed it just as much, if not more, than the one so thoughtfully planned and prepared for.

Sometimes we wonder if our efforts in this world—whether at home, at work, with friends, in church, or in the many other endeavors we pour ourselves into—will bloom (Galatians 6:9–10). When I don't see the results I hope for, I often wonder if "squirrels" came right behind me, digging up and destroying my efforts. And sometimes, they do. But other times, my little efforts—the single hour I offered as a volunteer, the simple meal or quick hug I gave, the small check I wrote to an organization—grow beyond all reasonable expectations. Sometimes we won't even see our efforts blossom in the people and organizations we pour our hearts into. Instead, those people will love others, who will love others, and that faith and love will bloom several stages down the road (1 Corinthians 15:58).

The body of Christ is both orderly and planned and a crazy quilt of unexpected joys and blossoms. There's a particular pleasure in watching both gardens realize their beauty, so keep planting.

Sow your seed in the morning, and at
evening let your hands not be idle, for you do
not know which will succeed, whether this or
that, or whether both will do equally well.
ECCLESIASTES 11:6

DAY 16
Bread Basket

You know that old joke, "I know what to make for dinner: reservations"? Having someone else make the food, serve the food, and clean up after is an absolute dream.

Many of the restaurants we visit serve a little appetizer: maybe chips with salsa or a basket of bread with dipping oils. One favorite eatery serves hot rolls drenched in garlic butter. Or sometimes it's biscuits with butter and jam or cornbread with honey. The best part? They'll refill the bread basket as many times as you want. For free!

Therein lies the problem, and I'm not just talking carbs. The meal still lies ahead.

By the time the delicious dinner arrives, we're full. We stick our forks in our entrees and take a few bites, but the food doesn't taste as good as we remembered. The bread had seemed like a treat at the time, but because we ate so much of it, we have no room left for the nourishing parts of our meals.

This happens in our spiritual lives, too. We fill ourselves up on TV, movies, books, or social media, using up our time and even our daily dose of concentration. By the time we turn our attention to God's Word—well, we're stuffed! Instead of having a little of the bread and a lot of the meal, we eat a whole basket of garlic rolls, and there's no room left for dinner.

Go ahead. Choose one biscuit: one TV show, something interesting on the Internet, or a few chapters of a great book. But be sure to save room for the main course every day (Psalm 119:103). I'm trying to consume less of the pre-meal entertainment so that I'll still be hungry for the Word of God (Matthew 4:4).

A person who is full refuses honey.
PROVERBS 27:7 NLT

Always in Hot Water

We were fortunate to buy a house built by a master plumber. He'd installed brushed-nickel fixtures and high-quality toilets. But the most exciting element to discover was the radiant heat installed throughout the house.

Radiant heat uses a large water heater in the garage to send hot water coursing constantly through yards and yards of tubing underneath the flooring. The heat rises and heats the entire room. Best of all? Warm feet when you pad about on a cold winter's morning.

But then it broke. We knew the system was expensive, so we prayed like mad that it would be repairable. Several hundred dollars for a fix seemed better than many thousands of dollars for a replacement. And after praying, I had peace about it. I just knew that it was going to be fixable. But it wasn't.

We got the bad news that the furnace needed to be replaced and that it would take a week—and a short-term loan—to do it. Later that evening, while waiting for an appointment, I kept praying. *Why didn't you just let it be repairable?* I asked God. *Or at least give us a big chunk of money to pay for it?*

As I sat there, praying and thinking, it came to me that when I pray, I often ask God to forestall bad things or, if it's too late for that, to provide an immediate fix. But neither of those requests really requires me to have faith that God will work things out for good, conforming us to the image of Christ (Romans 8:28–29). He will work for good in whatever circumstance appears on my horizon, whatever trouble I must undergo—and he usually does it in such a clever, creative, superhuman manner that there is no doubt it was God at work.

Hebrews tells us that without faith, we cannot please God. So why would He remove every opportunity we may have to please Him by trusting Him, to knit our hearts ever more tightly with His? He won't, which means we have plenty of time to build that love and faith while in the midst of the muddle.

Without faith it is impossible to please God, because anyone who comes to him must believe that he exists and that he rewards those who earnestly seek him.
HEBREWS 11:6

DAY 18
Drip Lines

After weeding, watering is the most arduous garden chore because you have to do it every day, or at least every other day. Once perennials are established, you can slack off a little . . . but not for long unless you want your beautiful greens and foliage to die.

One year we got smart—or lazy—and decided to install drip lines. It takes a little work up front—the preparation part—but then once it's established, all you have to do is turn on the faucet, and the plants get watered! If you're even lazier—er, smarter, like us—you can install a timer so you don't even have to remember to turn the water on. The plants get just what they need, constantly, a little drop at a time, so they are never dry nor flooded. They thrive. And we sit nearby drinking iced tea!

One day, while sipping said tea, I realized that those drip lines are like regular Bible study. It's best to get a little bit every day—not a flood, but enough to keep me hydrated. When I'm well-watered in the Word, I can withstand a day or two of scorching heat (Psalm 63:1). I can grow in spite of the circumstances. I'm healthy enough to deal with things that bedevil and pester me (Isaiah 26:3). The trick, of course, is to do the "setup work" in advance.

Do you have a time set aside each day in which you can read a few verses (Psalm 119:11)? How about listening to Scripture on audio during a walk or a commute? In gardening and in my spiritual disciplines, I've found that the easier I make it to follow through, the more likely I am to grow strong and thrive. God's Word never fails.

The LORD will guide you always; he will satisfy your needs in a sun-scorched land and will strengthen your frame. You will be like a well-watered garden, like a spring whose waters never fail.

ISAIAH 58:11

Marigolds and Bugbane

I was browsing garden forums online for advice about some plants I was considering purchasing when I came across a thread entitled "Plants you can't stand the smell of!" Who could pass up reading that?

Various plants were described as smelling like melted plastic, baby diapers (clean), garbage, onions, and rotting leaves. Bugbane can smell awful, like cat urine, which isn't surprising since its Latin name, *Cimicifuga*, means "bedbug repeller." I hope that is something I shall never have to find out for myself.

A plant I haven't yet grown, but which is very common, is marigold. I know its flowers are beautiful and long-lasting, but to me, they stink. I wouldn't like bending over to weed them, and I don't like walking by them on the path to my house. But they have that scent for the very same reason as bugbane—they repel pests. Once marigolds are in the garden, pests remove themselves from that area. The companion plants stay relatively untouched because of that. I admit: If I had pests in my garden, I'd plant marigolds. If I had bedbugs, I'd plant bugbane, too. No wise person turns away help (Proverbs 19:20)!

We, too, have pests in our lives; some of them are minor irritants, and one is a significant enemy. We have a Companion, though, who is much stronger than any of them, and He promises to keep us from evil. He's "planted" right next to us, wherever we are, watching over us. Yes, pests may circle, and they may land. They may even take a nibble or two, which hurts, certainly. But they will never ultimately destroy us (Romans 8:38) because we're protected from evil.

The LORD will keep you from all evil;
he will keep your life.
The LORD will keep
your going out and your coming in
from this time forth and forevermore.
PSALM 121:7-8 ESV

Cracked Pots

How much did you pay for that?" My husband gestured toward the terra-cotta pot I'd just scored from a yard sale.

"Ten dollars."

"It's cracked! And it has green stuff growing up the side!" He looked at me as if he were revealing new and potentially distressing information.

"I know," I replied, grinning. "Isn't it great? Patina!"

Now, we'd watched enough episodes of *Antiques Roadshow* together that I knew he understood the concept. Patina is the wear and tear on objects that comes from age and use. Some novice collectors attempt to remove the patina from their antique finds—bad idea. Removing the patina actually removes some, if not most, of the piece's value. Patina verifies character and individuality; it speaks of the object's history and can even offer protection from the elements. My husband walked away, muttering something about putting a "patina" sign on all of his broken tools and holding a garage sale, but I was satisfied. I liked the character my new pot lent to my front porch, and I went on a hunt in the backyard for a plant to pot in it.

By some "random coincidence," I had that very week been considering the gray streak in my dark hair. Did it add character? Or make me look, prematurely, like someone's grandmother? Some other signs of age—crow's feet, laugh lines, or a less-even skin tone—aren't as simple to cover up. And yet . . . when I have a problem in life, those are the very signs on a mentor that mark, for me, the wisdom that informs her suggestions (Proverbs 31:26), guidance, and prayer (Job 8:8–10). The patina of wisdom offers protection from the harsh realities of life, reflecting triumph over trials endured and storms weathered. It grows with experience and becomes ever more lovely—and valuable—with the passage of time.

In a youth-obsessed culture, there's something freeing about saying no to some cosmetic redirections. Even in terra-cotta.

Gray hair is a crown of glory;
it is gained by living a godly life.
PROVERBS 16:31 NLT

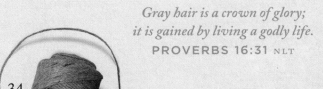

DAY 21
Wife Locator App

We had decided to divide and conquer the grocery list—I'd take the cart and the extensive list; my husband would go through the store looking for some specialty items. A memory of finding him wandering, looking up and down the rows for me, flashed through my mind. "Will you be able to find me?" I asked. He pulled out his phone. "Yes. I have now installed the Wife Locator, aka the Proverbs 31:10 app. 'A wife of noble character, who can find?' In other words, I'll just text, you'll answer, and I'll find you in no time."

Simple!

So often, I want to take the long, hard route. Well, I don't want to, but I end up doing so, mainly because I have an inherent belief that tells me, *It can't be as easy as that.* And yet, it often is.

The Lord is right by us, night and day. He says He will never leave nor forsake us. He intercedes for us. He is an ever-present help in times of trouble. So why do I wait so long to reach out and simply ask for help?

Maybe it's a matter of pride, busyness, or thinking the Lord is not concerned with the small stuff. Or perhaps it's unbelief. But to take Him at His word is to simply ask (Psalm 116:1–2). There's that old saying, "God always answers; sometimes He says yes, sometimes He says no." But for me, I've found that sometimes He says yes, and sometimes He says, "Here, let's try this instead." And it's always better.

I know how to use the God Locator app. I'll bet you do, too.

I say to you: Ask and it will be given to you; seek and you will find; knock and the door will be opened to you. For everyone who asks receives; the one who seeks finds; and to the one who knocks, the door will be opened.

LUKE 11:9–10

Love Covers a Multitude of Sins

In a house I lived in as a child, the bathroom wallpaper had been hung upside down. The pattern was intricate, so it was not quickly evident unless you were sitting there for some time with nothing to do but stare at the walls. Once you noticed it, however, it was easy to see that all of the little birds woven throughout the pattern were actually flying toward the ground, dive-bombing toward death, so it seemed. The bathroom decor was a constant source of amusement after that discovery.

I've hung some wallpaper in my own homes over the years, and while it isn't easy to do, I've found that it can be well worth the effort. Not only does the paper add texture, color, and design, it quickly and efficiently covers any defects on the wall. Perhaps there are dings or dents that a coat of paint simply can't conceal; wallpaper can. And hey, besides adding value and beauty to the room, the right paper can give you or your visitors something to stare at while sitting there for a time, doing nothing.

In my early Christian life, I'd always heard the verse "Love covers a multitude of sins" misused, as in, "I've sinned against you, but I don't feel like owning it. Because you're a Christian and supposed to love me, that love should cover any sin I've committed against you, or else you're unforgiving." Um, no. Here's what it does mean. We are humans; we err and have bad days when we make bad calls. We sin against others. But if *we* ask for *their* forgiveness and show them that we mean it by our subsequent actions (Luke 17:4), our sin is usually papered right over by our sincere desire—and our love—to make things right. In a healthy relationship, love always has the dents and dings covered. So love, and love well!

Most important of all, continue to
show deep love for each other,
for love covers a multitude of sins.
1 PETER 4:8 NLT

Ivy in the Walls

Ever since reading the children's book *Madeline*, I have been enchanted by the look of vines growing on a house. Vines make a house look sophisticated and beautiful, aristocratic somehow. When we moved into a new house with a broad face, I knew just how to accentuate that. Vines! I did some research and found the name of a vine I loved, one that was green in the summer and copper in autumn. Then I asked some friends, "Does anyone know anything about growing Virginia creeper?"

"Don't do it!" most of them told me. "Yes, yes, beautiful—all right, we'll give you that. But it is so invasive that you will never get it out once started. It not only grows along the face of your house, but in the cracks, under the siding (which loosens it up), and into the window casements (which makes them leak). You may pull, and you may spray, but once it's there, it's the owner, and you're the tenant."

So I changed my plans—no Virginia creeper. I'd known that it was strong—that a simple ivy could, over time, strangle a tree. I had not thought it was strong enough to rip my home apart. But it was.

Sin, it seems to me, works like that in our lives. It presents itself as something desirable and beautiful—or at the very least, harmless (Genesis 3:6). So I invite it in, welcoming whatever excitement it seems to bring my way—till it starts to wreak the havoc it always does (James 1:15). If I catch it in time, I can rip it out before it does harm. But that's not always possible. The best thing is not to plant it at all and avoid the pain it will most surely bring.

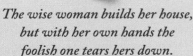

The wise woman builds her house, but with her own hands the foolish one tears hers down.
PROVERBS 14:1

Weeds Hiding

My new pink fountain plant had taken off, and I was thrilled. It was the third plant I'd placed in that exact spot, but it was the only one to thrive there. It was time to trim back its lush loveliness, though, and I found something unexpected when I did. A large weed, hiding behind it, had completely entangled itself in the roots of the fountain plant. The weed had taken refuge within the foliage of the desirable plant but was sucking up its nutrients, and that back section of the plant had started to die. I carefully pulled it all out: the large weed, the weed suckers, and all the roots I could find.

Most of us mean well, have good intentions, and do good deeds. And yet . . . we still sin. The places I'm most vulnerable are where I've been meeting with some success—where pride can sprout right alongside godly accomplishments—or places where I haven't taken root at all—where envy or bitterness grow (Proverbs 14:30). Sometimes all those good deeds I, or others, do, hide the sin behind a pretty façade. Eventually, if we let them, sins choke out the pleasure, joy, and good that our wholesome works produce. In the plant world and in life, weeds take root faster, grow stronger, and spread more easily than desirable plants. However, they are easier to handle when I pull them out regularly.

I love this section of Psalm 139 because it indicates that the psalmist's anxious thoughts spring from the concern that he may have offended God. He asks God to search his heart, to have a look and see if there is anything offensive, and if so, to show him how to uproot it. He's not anxious about things he doesn't have or things he may lose, but rather, his anxiety stems from his desire to keep himself righteous before God. I feel confident this is a prayer that He always answers.

Search me, God, and know my heart;
test me and know my anxious thoughts.
See if there is any offensive way in me,
and lead me in the way everlasting.
PSALM 139:23–24

The Three Sisters

The Iroquois people describe squash, beans, and corn as three sisters who can't be separated if they are to grow and thrive, often referring to the three plants as the "sustainers of life." When planted side by side in the same mound, the three plants help one another out; they are known as companion plants. Bean plants are vines—they need something sturdy to wrap around. The corn provides a tall pole for the beans to grow on. Once they do, they act like a rope, helping to anchor the cornstalks against the wind. Beans also put nutrients into the soil that the squash needs to thrive. Squash plants have prickly leaves and stems that repel animals that would otherwise nibble on the growing plants, and so they protect the beans and corn as well. Working together, all three plants can flourish and grow into an abundance of good eating.

There are three "sisters" in our Christian lives that work together, too (1 Thessalonians 1:2–3); where you find one, you're likely to find the others as they are interwoven and companionable. They help each other grow strong. Scripture tells us that these three things—faith, hope, and love—will last forever. Perhaps it would not be too far off to say that, for the believer, they are the sustainers of life.

Many of us have a little more of one or two of these than the other. For me, faith and love come more easily than hope. But if I carefully water and weed my heart, I find that the third sister can grow tall and strong, too. They need one another to thrive.

Do you have more faith, more hope, or more love? How can you feed and water the one or two that need a little boost to grow? What can you do to stake up the one that needs a little help?

Three things will last forever—faith, hope,
and love—and the greatest of these is love.
1 CORINTHIANS 13:13 NLT

Of Fruit and Flowers

For most plants, the right time to prune is just after they have flowered. It's lovely to enjoy the display of their floral glory, but if you wait too long to prune, you risk clipping off next year's blooms. For many plants, those blooms and the tips of the branches some of them grow on are not visible to the eye till the following season. But the plants begin to set their buds within a short time, so you can't procrastinate with pruning.

In one sense, it's fantastic to know that there will be another showy season to enjoy the following year. In another sense, it's hard to bring yourself to cut a plant back when a few vibrant blooms are still clinging to it. The willingness to make careful, timely cuts, though, allows the new display.

After we have come through a period of success—whether in ministry or our careers, with our families or friends—we're often tentative, waiting, as it were, for something bad to happen. And it always does, eventually, because life on earth is not one sustained high experience after the next. There are always valleys; there are always seasons of pruning. Perhaps the error lies in the perspective. It's not the end of a good run. To prepare us for another season, the Lord is clipping back what has already been productive and fruitful but is now spent (Hebrews 12:11).

Most gardeners know that to provoke more blossoms and more fruit (John 15:8) in the coming seasons, good pruning is required. Our Master Gardener can be trusted to clip gently, carefully—but clip He will. And we desire to blossom, to bear fruit, right? So it can be no other way.

He cuts off every branch in me that bears no fruit, while every branch that does bear fruit he prunes so that it will be even more fruitful.
JOHN 15:2

Pound Cake and Cookies

When my husband and I were seriously dating, I hoped to impress his mother by making her a birthday cake. Let's just say my husband didn't have a lot of good baking equipment, and I was not a very good baker at that time. The first cake ended up completely burnt. Acrid smoke filled the apartment, and the smell lingered no matter how many windows we opened. We ran out and bought a cake, which worked, till my future sister-in-law found the burnt cake hidden in a kitchen cupboard. What gave it away? I'm guessing the smell of death.

I went on to make more cakes, learning as I went, and today there is nothing that says "home" to me quite as much as a pound cake. Vanilla, butter, sugar, warmth—all of it spreading from kitchen to house to heart. I recently read that to sell houses more quickly, some real estate agents suggest baking cookies just before an open house. People smell that fragrance and think, *I want to live there!*

The apostle Paul's second letter to the Corinthians explains that believers are fragrant, too, and that fragrance extends everywhere. To those who are perishing, we bring an aroma of death with us. Not because we're bad, and hopefully not because we're critical or judgmental, but perhaps because when we come into a situation, we bring the Spirit with us, and He convicts. To our fellow Christians, we bring that same Spirit, and He reaches between us to bond, build fellowship, and remind us of our shared heritage and future (1 Thessalonians 5:11).

I believe with all my heart that heaven will be perfect, and therefore there must be pound cake and chocolate chip cookies waiting for us. I'm truly excited to have eternity to indulge in them (calorie free?) with my sisters and brothers in Christ.

We are to God the pleasing aroma of Christ among those who are being saved and those who are perishing. To the one we are an aroma that brings death; to the other, an aroma that brings life. And who is equal to such a task?
2 CORINTHIANS 2:15-16

DAY 28
Sin Resistant

I'm amused by the picture on some of the plant picks at my nursery. They show a doe with a "deer in the headlights" look on her face and a big red circle with a strike drawn through it. The language on the back of the pick is careful to note, though, that the plant is deer "resistant" and not deer "proof." No plant is entirely deer-proof, no matter how much we'd wish it to be. So we plant carefully and build an environment that at least makes our garden less desirable to what would damage or destroy it.

As we grow as people, as Christians, the sins that so easily ensnared us early in our walk with the Lord seem distant and much less of a temptation (Hebrews 12:1). We've replaced their dark and dangerous false pleasures with wholesome, righteous ones. And yet, we still inhabit our bodies of clay, our very human flesh, so none of us will stop sinning till the day we die. The book of 1 John tells us that to think otherwise would be to deceive ourselves and make God out to be a liar (1 John 1:10). None of us is sin-proof yet!

Since that is true, we can try, instead, to make a good environment for ourselves and others, planting our gardens and theirs with habits that make us resistant, at least, to sin. Surrounding myself with good books; spending time with people who love God and love others; listening to and sharing music that is uplifting and upbeat (Philippians 4:8–9); and sharing entertainment, pleasure, and fellowship with like-minded sisters and brothers (Philippians 3:17) builds me up rather than tempts me toward that which tears down.

It's more fun this way, too. Everything to gain, nothing to lose.

Well, my brothers and sisters, let's summarize. When you meet together, one will sing, another will teach, another will tell some special revelation God has given, one will speak in tongues, and another will interpret what is said. But everything that is done must strengthen all of you.
1 CORINTHIANS 14:26 NLT

Here, Kitty

One night my husband and I were slumped on the couch watching TV when an unusual advertisement caught my attention. A woman in her nightdress, squinting to see clearly, walked out onto the patio outside her bedroom to call for her cat. "Here, kitty," she called, and shortly, a big, gray raccoon padded past her. "Oh, there you are. Come snuggle with Mama," she said, not realizing that it was not her pet but a mean old predator making its way into her house and onto her bed. The commercial was for eyewear; bad things happen if you can't see clearly. As a result, you can unwittingly let trouble into your home and perhaps even your bed.

My family has had our share of run-ins with raccoons: They mess up your garbage if your lid isn't tight. They're happy to eat your pet's food—or even your pets—if you don't keep an eye on them. They spread disease. You don't want them in or around your house.

Sin can work its way into our homes in the same way when we do not see clearly. Sometimes we don't know that we do not see well, but sometimes, we deliberately leave the glasses off because we don't *want* to see better. Some "patio doors" that allow sin entrance into our lives and homes are apps, television, the Internet, music, books, indulging our flesh, and social media. It could enter through the books and magazines we read or the thoughts and people we entertain even when we know it would be better if we didn't (Genesis 4:7). Sin slips in looking like something welcome and then wreaks havoc once inside. It might be wiser to put on your glasses and lock the patio door (Job 31:1)!

My child, don't lose sight of common sense and discernment.
Hang on to them,
for they will refresh your soul.
They are like jewels on a necklace.
They keep you safe on your way,
and your feet will not stumble.
You can go to bed without fear;
you will lie down and sleep soundly.
PROVERBS 3:21-24 NLT

The Power of Deep Roots

One of my favorite flowers is the lily of the valley. I think it all started when I was a girl, and one of my first bottles of perfume was Tinkerbell's Lily of the Valley. I love that the blooms are delicate, parchment-thin bells that clump and perfume an entire area, sometimes even hiding under trees or shrubs. They aren't easy to start growing, but once started, they're tough little plants that hang on because their roots grow sideways. If you cut the plant off or even dig it up and move it, you likely will still have lily of the valley nearby the following year. Once established, they are persistent and strong.

Faith is sometimes like that, isn't it? When we're new believers, we're excited (Luke 19:1–10), but we've just begun to sprout from the seed of our faith, and Scripture tells us we can go wrong in several ways. A joyful embracing of faith can be short-lived when followed by trouble and persecution. Perhaps this life's worries (the omnipresent weeds) or the deceitfulness of wealth choke it off (Matthew 13). Maybe, on the other hand, the seed of faith settles into fertile soil, becomes established, and grows to maturity (Colossians 2:6–7).

But once it is established, our faith can resist those other troubles. We may face trauma (I once ran over my lily of the valley with a lawn mower!) and yet be able to spring back, a little damaged but stronger than ever. I don't know what troubles and worries and difficulties you face, but I do know that your roots can be strong and sturdy and persistent. You are rooted and established in love and firmly planted; you're unmovable, unshakable; you can't be mowed down because you understand how strong the love that sustains you is. It's long and high and deep, and it's all yours.

I pray that you, being rooted and
established in love, may have power,
together with all the Lord's holy people,
to grasp how wide and long and high and
deep is the love of Christ.
EPHESIANS 3:17–18

A Dish Called Patience

I've heard that revenge is a dish best served cold. I can't attest to that, having never served it to the best of my knowledge. I do serve up a lot of patience, though, every Easter. I have twelve servings of Patience—or, I should say, twelve place settings.

When I was a young woman, I took a job in a department store. I do not advise doing this: for every dollar I earned there, I spent two—even with my employee discount. One thing I set my heart on early in my employment was a set of fine Noritake china in a pattern called Patience. I wanted Noritake because it was my grandmother's brand; I wanted Patience because I had little of my own.

In those years, I wanted everything "right now." I wanted an answer to a prayer, the right boyfriend, the perfect job, a great car. I had little time to sit around while others did things that I thought I could do more quickly. Even as I grew older, I often rushed in to do it "right," which hurt feelings and damaged relationships. After a few of these chipped plates, so to speak, I learned to slow down. Plates may be replaced; relationships often cannot be.

Showing love for others is understanding that they operate differently than I do; their comfort levels might not be the same as mine. I am a planner; they may be spontaneous. I may like to speak up and solve problems quickly; they may like to think things through first. I came to understand that love for others meant holding my peace till they felt ready to move forward. Patience is waiting—peacefully, quietly, expectantly—on those we love: God and others. Patience can't be bought. It has to be cultivated, one circumstance at a time (James 1:4).

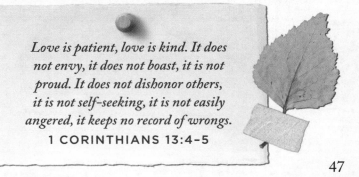

Love is patient, love is kind. It does not envy, it does not boast, it is not proud. It does not dishonor others, it is not self-seeking, it is not easily angered, it keeps no record of wrongs.

1 CORINTHIANS 13:4–5

Dripping Water

One day, I stepped onto the back porch and saw just one wet spot on the dry, cobbled path. When I examined it, I saw it was a moist cobblestone standing alone; the concrete grout around it had been completely worn away. A drainpipe clogged with debris had focused a stream of tiny, persistent drips on that small area. Over time those little drops, each no bigger than a sunflower seed, had worn away the tough, cured concrete.

The power of little drops. Water, it's been said, carved the Grand Canyon. Water smooths huge, sharp rocks into the round pebbles we walk on at the beach. It breaks those stones into even smaller particles of sand. Water—a little at a time, over a long period of time—can break down even the sturdiest material.

Remembering something about a leaking roof in Scripture, I sat down in my comfy chair and looked it up. Proverbs says that a quarrelsome wife is like the dripping of a leaky roof (Proverbs 27:15). I had always imagined how annoying that would be. A dripping bathroom faucet will make even a tired person haul out of bed to shut it off. But I had never thought about the destruction that those annoying drips could cause.

The verse talks about a wife, but I've also been annoyed by (and have annoyed, I am sure) quarrelsome people outside of a marital relationship. There are times to gently pursue a topic or conversation, and there are times to simply let it go. I need to remember to ask myself, *Will this matter in three days? Is this a persistent problem or a one-off? Am I just overtired? Is she?* It might not be my responsibility or prerogative to drip drip drip my advice or insight. Instead of building others up, our well-meaning words can break them down.

Love is not easily provoked, I'm reminded (1 Corinthians 13:5). And perhaps love does not easily provoke, either. It's much easier to shut off that faucet or clear the gutter than it is to fill in a Grand Canyon between someone I love and me.

Do not let any unwholesome talk come out
of your mouths, but only what is helpful for
building others up according to their needs,
that it may benefit those who listen.
EPHESIANS 4:29

DAY 33
Solar Powered

I was pushing my cart down the wide aisle of the big-box store when they caught my eye. Eight outdoor lights, solar-powered, would make the perfect finishing touch to the small path alongside our driveway. After a minute of mental math, I returned the French macaroons ($14) and a magazine ($6), so I could add the $20 lights to my haul.

Once home, I measured out the exact spacing, installed the lights, and waited. It was an unusually sunny day, so I hoped they would charge quickly and be on display that very night. "When do they come on?" my son-in-law asked. "As soon as it's dark," I answered. But that night, they did not.

"Maybe they need more time to charge?" I asked my husband. He shook his head, went outside, and took the plastic sticker off the top of each one. The overlooked stickers, it seems, had been blocking the lamps' ability to take in the sunlight.

The next day the lamps charged right up. As soon as dusk fell to darkness, each light blinked on. Delighted, I ran outside to see that yes, they *were* the perfect touch and lit up the path nicely.

Scripture tells us that from the very beginning, God did not leave us in the dark either physically or spiritually (Genesis 1:14–16; Psalm 119:105). At night the moon, of course, reflects the sun's light, and my solar lights absorb the sun's energy and release it, as it were, when it's dark.

I love the play on words and concepts—absorbing the light of the Son and releasing it when it's darkest. Each of us has dark moments; even some of Jesus's friends rejected Him, His family thought He was unbalanced (Mark 3:21), the leaders of the time hated Him, and He had nowhere to lay His head (Luke 9:58).

"Don't forget in the darkness what you learned in the light," Christian author Joseph Bayly exhorts. The key, I believe, is taking off whatever barriers prevent you from absorbing and storing sunlight during the best of days so you have power reserves when darker times arrive.

In him was life, and that life was the light of
all mankind. The light shines in the darkness,
and the darkness has not overcome it.

JOHN 1:4–5

Locusts

A few years ago, the people of a small farming town near where a friend grew up watched as a giant, black cloud moved menacingly close. Suddenly, the buzzing cloud dropped to the ground, and millions of locusts began chewing up any and all living plants—stalks of grass, dandelions, and worst of all, the carefully tended wheat crop. Imagine the menacing hum of those jaws devouring a year's worth of the farmers' work. The bug-covered roads seemed to move. Like the Red Sea, the insects would part only when a car (with its windows tightly rolled up) would drive through.

As quickly as they came, the bugs departed, but only when nothing was left to eat. The land was completely mowed down, the air stank, and gloom hovered over the devastation. The farmers had no harvest that year. They were discouraged, scared, and broke. We've all been there, haven't we? All our hopes and dreams chewed up by circumstances completely beyond our control.

The following winter was so cold that most of the grasshopper eggs did not survive. When summer came, the crops grew thick, and that autumn brought the most marvelous harvest ever—enough to make up for everything that had been lost the year before. Because there had been a crop shortage the previous year, the prices were higher, which meant more income (1 Peter 5:10).

What hard things have happened in your life that you are discouraged about? Do you believe that God is willing and able to restore them when the time is just right, even when you stand among the ruins? Hold on because a year of harvest will soon follow. He promises.

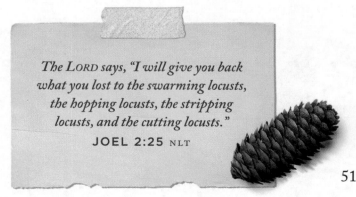

The LORD says, "I will give you back what you lost to the swarming locusts, the hopping locusts, the stripping locusts, and the cutting locusts."
JOEL 2:25 NLT

Mold

We live in a region where damp is a state of being at least six months out of the year. Our clothes are moist from running in and out of the car and in and out of buildings (umbrellas are for tourists!), rugs are damp from wet shoes, and the dog sometimes smells like, well, wet dog. The back patio, overshadowed by trees, never really catches any sun, not even in the summer. The cobblestones making up the patio are now a beautiful gray, aged and lovely, but we didn't spend any time on the patio for a long time because the stones were slippery and slick with green. They didn't smell good. Back there, where they were, it was not only damp, it was dark. Here's something I learned: Mold grows in the dark.

To get rid of the mold, we not only had to dry things up, but we also had to lighten them up. Once the tree branches were trimmed way back and the cobblestones were exposed to the sunlight, the mold began to dry up and wither till, eventually, I could vacuum it off. It did not return. The sun had made this possible. No more slipping and sliding when walking outdoors!

There is mold in our lives, too. The parts of us that we don't want to grow, that aren't healthy, that we believe to be ugly—well, they thrive in the dark. We keep secret the things we consider to be shameful about ourselves. Would our friends still love us if they knew? Would we be taken out of a ministry?

The truth is that light heals, light strengthens, light brings life (Ephesians 5:8–10). Start small—open up a little corner of vulnerability to someone you trust. Just sharing a little bit will lighten your load, and before you know it, that shame will be vacuumed away!

I have come into the world as light,
so that whoever believes in me may
not remain in darkness.
JOHN 12:46 ESV

Fruitful and Withering Branches

The sky was that clear blue peculiar to autumn—or maybe the sky just looks bluer against the dry, wheat-colored grass it bumps up against. In any case, it was a perfect day for a drive to a local fruit stand. My dessert menu was ready to move on from berries to apples and other autumn fruit!

After parking, I noticed a wild pear tree next to the little market. Its branches were absolutely burdened with fruit, and the sweet, ripe scent drew not only me but also some yellow jackets. I walked as close as I dared. Although the tree wasn't carefully tended, it was lush; the weight of the pears pulled the branches toward the ground—easy pickings. There were even pears growing on the suckers sprouting from the tree's base.

We made a purchase, and then I took my haul home and wandered out to the backyard, where I'd just begun to dig up the summer squash plants. I'd plucked a vibrant yellow squash blossom the night before, but now it wilted, withering, and beginning to go brown and dry. If I had left it attached to the squash vine, could I have had just one more squash? I thought so.

Anything connected to the main plant continues to bear fruit, like the abundance of pears I'd seen earlier, sometimes even without careful tending. But once removed from the life source, like my squash blossom, it begins to die and decay immediately, useless but for kindling. I walked back into my office, where I dedicated myself anew to staying connected with God and wanting to overflow with good fruit. I placed my Bible where I'd see it each morning and programmed worship music into my playlist. I didn't want to end my day, or my life, disconnecting from the Vine.

I am the vine; you are the branches. If you remain in me and I in you, you will bear much fruit; apart from me you can do nothing. If you do not remain in me, you are like a branch that is thrown away and withers; such branches are picked up, thrown into the fire and burned. If you remain in me and my words remain in you, ask whatever you wish, and it will be done for you. This is to my Father's glory, that you bear much fruit, showing yourselves to be my disciples.

JOHN 15:5-8

DAY 37
Claiming a Stake

I love topiary (see devotion 7). I have fun little silk boxwood twists inside the house, and I wanted some living topiary outside, too. So one year I bought four for the front yard: two pink Tinkerbelle lilacs, a fragrant white camellia, and a yellow witch hazel. Part of the topiary charm is the slender stalk upon which rests a large, tousled head of untamed leaves and puffs of flower. That flexible stalk, though, is weak for several years, often the result of having been grafted onto the rootstock of a hardier plant.

My house faces a windy bluff, and therefore my lovely little topiaries needed a helping hand. I put thin stakes into the ground and then used landscape fabric to tie the topiary trunks to those stakes. The supports gave my plants backbones, if you will, to help them withstand the first few years in the ground while they adjusted to their new home.

A master gardener warned me to remove the stakes after a number of years, just before autumn winds begin to blow. If I didn't, the plant would remain weak and dependent upon the stakes, unable to grow the strong roots and thick trunk required to face those winds on its own. Developing the strength to stand firm and withstand the storms would help it live long and prosper. I felt a little nervous at first when I removed the stake and waited for the first sustained winds. Would the plant snap? It did not. It stood straight, tall, and firm.

That seems like a good analogy for all those we train, teach, and mentor. Whether they be our children or students, or even when we are being mentored, the idea is not to grow dependent upon the stake but to rely on it while we get strong. And then take the stake away. Once strengthened, we can face those winds on our own.

I will instruct you and teach you in the way you should go;
I will counsel you with my loving eye on you.

PSALM 32:8

DAY 38
Sowing and Reaping

Our lawn was balding quicker than, well, quicker than someone who lives at our house and shall remain unnamed. Bald is beautiful, though! Unless it's your yard.

So we decided we'd reseed it, taking advantage of the autumn rains and trying the cheaper route before investing in sod. First, we had to kill the weeds and remove them. Then, we scattered grass seed. After that, we rolled over the yard with a prickly machine designed to push the seeds into the ground, splitting the seeds as it did. Weeks later, thin, green blades of grass began threading their way up through the soil. Our new lawn looked to be a success.

As we washed off that seed-piercing machine to store it away, I thought about Scripture. The book of John tells us that unless a grain of wheat dies, it remains alone; it cannot grow or reproduce. Tertullian, an early church father, proclaimed that "the blood of the martyrs is the seed of the church." We live in a time when it seems that there is more global violence against people in general, including Christians dying for their faith. We know that there would be no salvation for any of us without shed blood (Hebrews 9:22). The word *martyr* means "witness," and those who die for the name of Christ are witnessing their faith in this reality; a more powerful testimony cannot be found.

The Lord still calls, "Can I get a witness?" to some. Let's pray today for those courageous enough to answer, "Here I am, Lord. Send me" (see Isaiah 6:8).

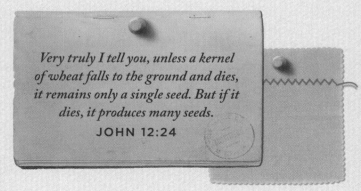

Very truly I tell you, unless a kernel of wheat falls to the ground and dies, it remains only a single seed. But if it dies, it produces many seeds.
JOHN 12:24

On Display

We had befriended a young couple; one of them had family members who'd been mired in paganism and other dark practices. As this couple began to turn more and more toward the Son, they simultaneously experienced more and more spiritual attacks and oppression. Many times we prayed with them, and they grew stronger. Yet when we left their home, we often felt like we were leaving them vulnerable, unattended in a shadowy neighborhood.

One time shortly after we'd left, the Lord reminded me that our friends were not unattended; He himself remained (Deuteronomy 31:8), as did the angels Scripture tells us are sent to minister to those who will inherit salvation (Hebrews 1:14). I wanted these friends to have a tangible reminder of that, day and night. The Spirit brought to mind that this couple, who lived on a tight budget, did not have a cross in their home.

I had one. But it was my *special* cross. It had been a gift from a group of people I work with, made from stone quarried in Jerusalem. It was mounted on a wall in a location I walked by often. It was a treasure to me, like He whom it represented. I had even told the young couple about the cross and its significance to me.

I wanted to give it to them. And yet, I did not want to. As I stood in front of it, I thought: *The cross was not meant primarily to be displayed, whether on our walls or around our necks, but to be given away.*

We took the cross down from the wall, drove to that couple's home, and gave it to them; they were overjoyed. They hung it on a prominent wall in their own home. As we drove away, I was glad that the Holy Spirit had nudged me to act and that I'd been obedient to follow His instruction—something I don't always do.

I trust that in the right way, at the right time, I will find another cross to treasure. The spot on my wall remains bare but for the nail, which reminds me of the true cost of sacrifice.

Do not withhold good from those who deserve it
when it's in your power to help them.
PROVERBS 3:27 NLT

Slow Leak

Throughout the winter, I had become very sick to my stomach several times. I had no other symptoms of illness, so the diagnosis was stress. A month or two later, a member of my family who had never been prone to headaches began to have them fairly regularly. Cause assigned? Stress.

Spring came, and with the sunshine, our symptoms cleared up. Or so we thought. Once it grew cooler out and we turned on the heat again, the symptoms returned. Diagnosis? There was a slow leak in our furnace; the gas had been leaking into the house, making us sick. Eventually, it could have caused someone to die.

The gas was odorless and tasteless, and initially, the meter designed to detect it didn't sense it. But our bodies were telling us something was wrong, even though we couldn't pinpoint just what it was at first; it took time and discernment. I thought about how much this is like other situations I sometimes find myself in. Things may seem natural and good at the outset, but along the way, I begin to sense that something just isn't right. Over time, as I begin to suffer the consequences—in body, spirit, and mind—my eyes are opened, and I discern the problem (John 16:13). The spiritual *aha* moment. Once I see the problem, I must either fix the problem or forsake the situation.

So often, we start with good intentions—a job, a ministry, a church, a relationship—but then, along the way, it becomes clear that something is wrong. Perhaps the people turn out to be other than who they had represented themselves to be; the job requires you to bend your ethics or morals, if not the law; a relationship is toxic (there's a reason for that phrase), or the ministry takes more than you have to give or does not advance the cause of Christ. Once the Spirit leads us to the diagnosis, the problem must be remedied or the situation abandoned! And then . . . you will be well again.

Do not be misled: "Bad company corrupts
good character."
1 CORINTHIANS 15:33

High-Powered Blowers

D o you know about high-powered blowers? I do. We bought a leaf blower when we moved into our first house. I used it every autumn to corral those pesky leaves into a pile for the dog to frolic through and for us to bag up and compost. We also use it to blow the dust from our driveway and walkways. I never had huge piles of dirt to blow away, but I ended up covered in a fine shroud of dust whenever I used the machine. Of course, the place I aimed the machine at was clean and clear, but one look at me, and you'll know what I've been up to.

People who speak ill of others are not so different from high-powered blowers. They may think they are spreading juicy nuggets of gossip or casting doubt on another's character, but mainly they are drawing attention to their own weakness—the dirt sticks to the one who spreads it. And they're not winning any friends; if they gossip to you when no one else is present, they'll gossip *about* you when you're not there—and who needs a "friend" like that?

I used to think I had to defend myself from those who had blown dirt my way. Now I know I don't need to. Instead, I work hard to keep my own mouth and motives pure, knowing that character speaks louder than words (2 Corinthians 3:2–3). If I don't gossip and my behavior reflects the fruit of the Spirit, those who malign me will not be believed; their dust will stick to themselves (Proverbs 26:24–27). But if I join in blowing that hot air, then when ill is spoken of me, it will be easier to believe. It's hard not to stick up for yourself. But keeping silent isn't running scared. It's trusting that your integrity is known and seen.

Do not worry when others speak ill of you (1 Peter 2:12). Your own actions are your best defense.

> *Keep your conscience clear. Then if people*
> *speak against you, they will be ashamed*
> *when they see what a good life you live*
> *because you belong to Christ.*
> **1 PETER 3:16** NLT

Building Nests

O ne morning, I took a work break and sat on my back porch with an iced coffee, watching the birds flit about. Chirpy, cheerful birdsong early in the morning always heralds spring for me, and now I watched as my winged friends began to build their nests.

Theirs is very time-consuming work. The birds flutter to the ground, find twigs—not too heavy but big enough to add bulk—and then fly them back to the nest-in-progress. Back and forth, back and forth, for some time. Some were more diligent than others, and their nests were tighter, firmer, safer, and perhaps more comfortable. Finally, when the structure is complete, they've made something they would have to live in, for better or worse.

That week I had been nursing a grudge (what an apt word—*nursing!*) against someone who had hurt my feelings. Day by day, I would review things, in the privacy of my mind, that I thought helped build my case. She'd done this. She'd said that. She'd forgotten something else. I'd reach further and further for evidence to justify my resentment. But as I watched the birds that morning, I realized I had been building a nest of hurt, twig by twig—a home of bitterness and sorrow that I would have to live in.

I decided to call the other person, and we started a somewhat tricky conversation that ended with laughter and plans for the future (Hebrews 12:14). Just as a nest can be built twig by twig, it can be dismantled a piece at a time, too. The same is true of a grudge. It's much easier to nurse a grudge and make war with someone. But it's more life-giving to build peace.

Turn from evil and do good;
seek peace and pursue it.
PSALM 34:14

The Sweetest Scent

When my daughter grew up and moved out, she wanted one thing of mine to take with her. No, not a kitchen appliance or the vacuum cleaner (although she took some of those later). She wanted one of my old perfume bottles. The request brought tears to my eyes.

She was all grown up, and I was proud of my daughter, but I cherished the thought that even out on her own in the world, she would want to pop the top of one of my perfume bottles, inhale deeply, and feel that I was close.

I remember my first perfume: Love's Baby Soft. I loved it. When my daughter was old enough for perfume, I bought her some Love's Baby Soft, too, which she enjoyed. Of course, she and I don't wear the same scents anymore, but we each have found a fragrance that we love, and they have become our signature scents. She still keeps mine near, though she is a grown woman with her own family. Someday, she will give her daughter a small spritz bottle of Love's Baby Soft. It's still available!

Perfume played an essential role in the Bible, too. For example, just before Jesus was to be crucified, a woman poured costly perfume over Him to give Him honor. Another time, Mary Magdalene, a follower of Jesus, washed His feet with her tears, wiped them dry with her hair, and then rubbed expensive perfume on His feet, also to honor and thank Him.

God tells us that the knowledge of Christ is actually like a sweet perfume and that we, His followers, are to spread that wherever we go. In a sense, the discernible presence of Jesus is the signature scent of a Christian.

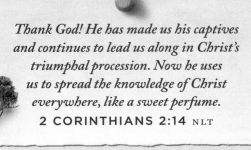

Thank God! He has made us his captives and continues to lead us along in Christ's triumphal procession. Now he uses us to spread the knowledge of Christ everywhere, like a sweet perfume.

2 CORINTHIANS 2:14 NLT

Let There Be Rest

I adore French style and French food, so I've tried to learn to cook and bake a few French treats, most with success. But I've struggled with croissants.

To get those flaky layers, the dough has to be given proper time to rest, or it will never become that buttery treat we enjoy.

We humans need rest, too. So often, we're on go-go-go, hounded by looming deadlines and bills. Every well-intentioned health care provider tells us more things we need to do to care for ourselves. Church wants more help for ministry. Work becomes more competitive, and we want to invest time in our relationships. And, oh, that social media drain! There is a temptation to skip the rest that God commands—the Sabbath.

The Sabbath is one day each week set aside for no work (Leviticus 23:3). I admit that I struggle to keep it—I have so many important things to get done! However, I was thumbing through verses on the Sabbath a few weeks ago and came upon the passage about how the women who had gone with Jesus to His crucifixion wanted to prepare His body for burial. Since it was the Sabbath, though, they waited till the next day.

Wait a minute. What do I have to do that is more important than what those women had to do? Really . . . nothing. And yet they obeyed the command to honor the Sabbath. They took God at His word, even when caring for . . . God.

The Lord knows that rest allows us to enjoy the life He has created for us and do our best work on the other days, and He has given us a day every week for just that purpose.

The women who had come with Jesus from
Galilee followed Joseph and saw the tomb
and how his body was laid in it. Then
they went home and prepared spices and
perfumes. But they rested on the Sabbath
in obedience to the commandment.

LUKE 23:55-56

Broken Vessels

I don't know where I first came across a piece of *kintsugi*, but it made an immediate impression, and from that moment on, I wanted to own some. Not just any piece of *kintsugi*, but a communion set, which made its symbolism even more poignant.

Kintsugi is the Japanese art of taking broken pottery and repairing it with seams of gold. The pottery itself is usually nothing spectacular—made of red clay, perhaps; small; fashioned by hand but without any features that call attention to it. However, each piece is one of a kind because the broken parts aren't covered up and hidden; instead, they are celebrated. The very fact that the piece has been broken and then made whole again with the most precious material is what gives each piece its unique beauty. The piece becomes more beautiful than when it was unbroken and common.

Isaiah prayed, "You, LORD, are our Father. We are the clay, you are the potter; we are all the work of your hand" (Isaiah 64:8). Sometimes the Lord allows circumstances to enter our lives, which break us, shatter us into pieces, and ruin our hope or our sense of usefulness and wholeness. But even then, we are not out of His hand. He takes us and mends us with the gold that is His love. The shattering and the mending are what make us unique. We are repaired by the gold of Christ (Ephesians 2:10 NLT), who himself was broken and mended.

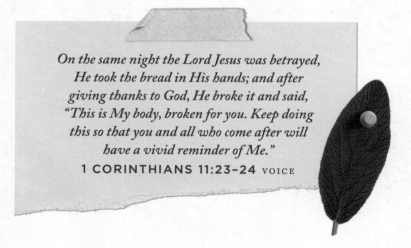

On the same night the Lord Jesus was betrayed,
He took the bread in His hands; and after
giving thanks to God, He broke it and said,
"This is My body, broken for you. Keep doing
this so that you and all who come after will
have a vivid reminder of Me."
1 CORINTHIANS 11:23-24 VOICE

DAY 46
Soft Sheets and Lumpy Pillows

I have always loved the idea of having a guest room in my home, but it hasn't been very many years that we've had the space to have one. So when I finally did have a guest room, it was exciting to prepare a room in which my beloved family and friends, visitors to our church, or people the Lord brought our way would be able to sojourn comfortably.

I set about painting it a warm but restful color and decorated it with an eye toward France—dried lavender, soft colors, and a side-by-side English and French Bible translation. Quiet clock? Check. A little dish of candies? Check. Linens for bathing? Check! The most important element, of course, was the bedding. I piled it on à la *The Princess and the Pea* so our guests would have a restful night's sleep.

After I finished preparing the room, a friend joked that perhaps we should add some lumpy pillows. After all, we didn't want people to become so comfortable that they never wanted to leave . . . right? Her comment reminded me of the years when our then-teenaged son would not get up on time in the morning, and we finally rolled some marbles under his sheets so that it would be more comfortable to get out of bed than to stay put.

We can become too comfortable in this world, too, which in actuality is not our home (Philippians 3:20). We are just passing through, strangers in the land, as Scripture puts it. Thérèse of Lisieux reminds us, "The world's thy ship and not thy home." God gives us many pleasant, comfortable things to help us see His goodness in the land of the living, but we mustn't become so comfortable that we don't want to depart someday for our true home.

This world is not our permanent home; we
are looking forward to a home yet to come.
HEBREWS 13:14 NLT

Cuttings and Transplants

A recent addition to my gardening arsenal is rooting hormone, a neat little liquid that helps plants transplant more easily; it gives the roots a healthy boost. You can use it two ways: If you want to replicate a plant you already have, especially vines like ivy, take a healthy cutting and then dip the end into the rooting hormone before planting. Second, if you buy a plant from a nursery or are gifted one from a friend, a little of this added to the initial watering will help it transition into its new home—in your yard!

As I dipped a few cuttings into the rooting hormone, it seemed to me that this is very much like introducing our friends to our faith. Christianity is an evangelizing faith; we're called to share the good news with others. Of course, we're not to duplicate ourselves but to be agents through whom the Holy Spirit works.

Sometimes when people are fresh in their faith, the new "territory" can seem a bit bewildering, and we don't want them to wither and die. So here's where the second use can come in handy. We've got to come alongside and make the ground hospitable! Cultivate the soil with love, so there's a soft landing for those who stumble. Water with kindness and attention; offer a hand, an ear, a prayer till they're rooted and beyond. It can be overwhelming to be transplanted from one kingdom to the next—we've all experienced it, haven't we? But what a pleasure and a privilege to come alongside the Gardener as He works.

Restore us, God Almighty;
make your face shine on us,
that we may be saved.

You transplanted a vine from Egypt;
you drove out the nations and planted it.
You cleared the ground for it,
and it took root and filled the land.

PSALM 80:7–9

DAY 48
Guardian Angels

A friend needed to babyproof her house, and among her biggest concerns were her second- and third-floor windows. The windows needed to open to allow for air circulation in the house. But an energetic toddler could push a screen right out, tumbling with it in the long drop to the ground. Together we searched the Internet and ultimately came upon a product called Guardian Angel Window Guards.

These nifty products screw into the sides of windows, barring the window with rods about three or four inches apart. The bars provide plenty of space for air to circulate but not enough room for a kid to squeeze through. Once we installed them, everyone was happy—life could go on comfortably in all seasons without the risk of a child being harmed. The window guards could be quickly installed and then forgotten, one less thing to worry about.

Many of us are enchanted by the idea of angels, especially a guardian angel or someone sent specifically to watch over us (Matthew 18:10). Christ himself watches over us, of course, but Scripture tells us that there are also heavenly beings God has commissioned to care for His people. Daniel had firsthand experience of this when he was in the lions' den. "My God sent his angel, and he shut the mouths of the lions," Daniel reported (Daniel 6:22). Perhaps you've heard modern-day stories of cars being lifted and assailants being repelled. As with anything in the spiritual realm, we do not completely understand how and when and why angels work. But they do—and that's part of the mystery of faith.

A good parent anticipates the difficulties and dangers that might befall her children and takes precautions to keep them safe. Isn't it comforting to know that your heavenly Father has also prepared others to serve and protect *you*?

Angels are only servants—spirits sent to
care for people who will inherit salvation.
HEBREWS 1:14 NLT

Transitions

It came time to replace the worn-out carpeting in our house, and we had such fun choosing and ordering the new flooring. After we had selected the new carpet and hardwood, the sales associate led us to another set of products. "What are these?" I asked. "Transitions," she said. "They go between the carpet and the wood, or between the wood and the tile, smoothing the way so that no one will trip and get hurt."

So we bought some transitions to bridge the gaps between the different flooring materials and had those installed, too. When everything was done, our floors were flawless, and the pathways were smooth. As I gave them one last approving look one night as I turned out the lights, I thought about a different set of transitions that move us from one stage of life to the next.

Honestly, I don't like them. It makes me nervous—and excited, too—when things change from one comfortable, familiar circumstance to the next unknown adventure. New job, new town, new church, new calling, new friends or family. I rarely know where to place my foot in the new venture, and I'm worried I'll make a misstep and tumble, maybe bringing someone down with me. I don't like to disappoint. I don't like to fail. But when God calls me forward into the unknown, there is almost always a risk; without risk, faith would not be required.

When Jesus calls us out upon the water, He holds out His hand and bids us keep our eyes on Him. He will not let us drown or sink, and faith in Christ will never lead to ultimate disappointment. We can trust Him through all of life's transitions because He is always the bridge who smooths and protects the way (Isaiah 26:7).

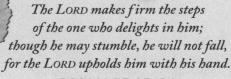

The LORD makes firm the steps
of the one who delights in him;
though he may stumble, he will not fall,
for the LORD upholds him with his hand.
PSALM 37:23-24

DAY 50
Stew

As I lifted the lid on the slow cooker, a meaty, aromatic cloud greeted me. Just that little bit evaporating into the winter air was enough to perfume the kitchen with cold-weather goodness. Earlier in the day, I had cut up inexpensive vegetables, meat, and potatoes and thrown all the pieces into the pot with some broth and herbs to simmer. Now the cuts were tender and ready to be served and enjoyed.

The taste of herbs and vegetables commingled with meat that melts in your mouth never fails to please. Esau sold his birthright for just such a bowl (Genesis 25:29–34); it's that good. So what transforms a relatively tough cut of meat into toothsome goodness? Constant heat over a long time.

When tough things happen in life, our first instinct is to resolve them quickly and make the pain disappear or pray for immediate relief. Sometimes, when relief doesn't come right away, I wonder if God is listening and if He really loves me. And if the answer is yes on both counts, well then, where is my rescue?

The apostle Paul tells us that circumstances that must have been difficult for him to endure over and over—time and heat—actually turned out, in the end, for his betterment and the advancement of the Kingdom. So next time I'm stewing over something, I might ask, *Is this making my rough cut tender? Am I willing to stick out difficult circumstances long enough for them to transform me?*

I want you to know, brothers and sisters, that
what has happened to me has actually served to
advance the gospel. As a result, it has become clear
throughout the whole palace guard and to everyone
else that I am in chains for Christ. And because of
my chains, most of the brothers and sisters have
become confident in the Lord and dare all the more
to proclaim the gospel without fear.
PHILIPPIANS 1:12–14

"What If" or "I AM"?

One of the best parts about decorating or remodeling is asking, "What if?"

"What if we move the couch over here?"

"What if we paint this room another color—or even just the ceiling?"

"What if we spend the Christmas bonus replacing that ratty carpet?"

All right, one person in the family likes what-if questions and one does not (the one who has to do the heavy lifting and thinks the couch is just fine where it is, thank you very much!).

Although there are many delightful what-if questions, many what-if questions that float through our hearts and minds are not so happy.

"What if the test comes back positive?"

"What if I lose my job?"

"What if my child walks away from his faith?"

"What if we lose our house?"

Many of us spend quite a bit of time and energy dwelling on those anxiety-provoking what-if questions, not the good ones about buying new bathroom rugs. The vagaries of life, ever-changing circumstances, and our absolute inability to control situations that could harm us or those we love—these all make us nervous. But there's a two-word antidote for the two-word problem.

I AM.

"I am big enough to walk through the test with you and, should the test come back positive, arrange for your healing on earth or here with me. I am capable of finding another job for you or providing for you in a unique way you may not have thought of. Your child is really my child, right? I am certain I've got this one. You will gain and lose and gain houses in this world. But my house has many rooms (John 14:2–3), and you can be sure that there will always be one for you."

The fun-to-think-about what-ifs are good for your mind, your heart, and your soul. The panicked ones, not so much. Remodel, renew, and replace with "I AM."

God said to Moses, "I AM WHO I AM."
EXODUS 3:14

A Time for Everything

I was outside raking—which was hearty exercise, and actually felt good—in a warm hoodie and amongst cold breezes. The sky was bright blue; the leaves fluttering down were shades of wine and gold. It was kind of sad that they were at their most beautiful on their way to death. I picked one up. It had lost its pliable nature and was becoming stiff and crispy. And yet what a way to go out, in a blaze of glory, which most of us (though we are not leaves) might choose to do as well (Ecclesiastes 7:8).

The thought struck me: the tree must release that which is dead or dying to bring new life in a new season. I have held on to jobs for too long, past the time when I knew I could be serving better elsewhere. I've stayed in relationships out of nostalgia, even when they were no longer healthy. I've retained habits that weren't working, and I have had to transition from mother of children to mother of adults, which is harder than it sounds. But without the ability and willingness to let go of that which has had its time (Philippians 3:13–14), I would not be able to make room for new people, new ministries, new phases—I'm a grandmother now!

Don't be afraid to let go of something whose time has passed. It can go out in a blaze of beautiful glory, long remembered and treasured. Letting go makes way for new buds, shoots, flowers, and leaves. As something old passes and something new takes its place, the tree grows year by year. And so do we.

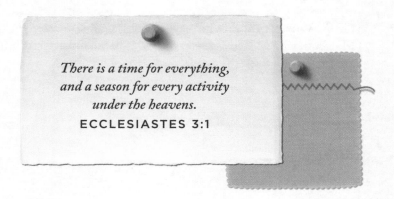

There is a time for everything,
and a season for every activity
under the heavens.
ECCLESIASTES 3:1

DAY 53
Making Things Palatable

My son's friend was joining us for dinner, and he announced that he absolutely could not eat the polenta and prosciutto I was serving that night. It sounded awful to him. "How about ham and grits?" I asked. "Sure," he replied, happy. Polenta versus grits, prosciutto versus ham—exactly the same foods, but renamed to make them palatable.

There was no harm done in this case, and we laugh about it to this day, but renaming things isn't always benign. One thing many of us are tempted to rename is sin. *He's not arrogant; he's moody. It's not a lie; it's stretching the truth. It's not wrath; it's a short temper.* We soft-pedal the sins of others because either we don't want to face the truth about those we love, or we're afraid to confront them. We change the names of our own sins because we don't want to own them. Owning our sins, we mistakenly believe, condemns us.

Sin stands between God and us, and His love and sacrifice make it clear that He desires to be near us and to have us draw near to Him. John 3:17 tells us that Jesus did not come into the world to condemn it but to save it. The term *confess*, a verb in the Greek (1 John 1:9), is a compound word that means to say the same thing, to agree with. In this case, it means to agree with God. Let's not sugarcoat our sin; let's not soft-pedal it. Confessing our sins does not condemn us—it saves us. It frees us not only for intimacy with our Lord but for intimacy with others we do not want to push away by our bad behavior. When we confess our sins, He forgives them, removing our guilt (Psalm 32:5) and that condemnation we so fear.

The way to reinstate intimacy is to own our sin, call it what it is, and humbly ask those who have sinned against us to own their sin, too (Matthew 18:15). Then, repentance is at hand, forgiveness is available, and often reconciliation is possible.

Woe to those who call evil good
and good evil,
who put darkness for light
and light for darkness,
who put bitter for sweet
and sweet for bitter.
ISAIAH 5:20

Anointed

One day, I was cleaning out the pantry and was amazed by the number of condiments, especially the oils, that I found therein. Sesame seed oil for Asian dishes, walnut oil for salads, apricot kernel oil, almond oil, canola oil, olive oil. The bottles sat quietly in the dark, waiting to be summoned into the bright kitchen for good use.

Throughout history, oil has been dear—costly—because it takes so much of something to produce just a teaspoon of the oil, the essence that is squeezed out of it. Extra virgin olive oil comes from the first press of the olive and is the purest, and therefore the most expensive, kind of olive oil. Oil has a long history of use in our faith, too, and some is a part of everyday use (Ezekiel 16:13; Exodus 27:20) and for purposes of faith (Exodus 30:25). We read in 2 Kings 4:1–7 that Elisha asked God for supernaturally provided oil for one of the widows of the prophets so she could pay her husband's debts and save her sons from slavery.

Oil can also represent the Holy Spirit. Luke 4 tells us that the Spirit of the Lord *anointed* Jesus, evoking images of kings, prophets, and priests who were anointed with precious oil. Like oil, the Spirit is dear and precious, and He came to humanity at a great price. Living within us, the Holy Spirit fills us with the essence of God.

Perhaps the most poignant use of oil is when Mary poured a pint of the essence of spikenard over Jesus's feet to show extreme honor and value. While Martha served (something we might do easily and willingly), Mary gave sacrificially in a way that others may have been embarrassed to do. And yet that gift perfumed the whole house and has lived on as an example of devotion.

I often think that my giving needs to fall into the same patterns: financial or time, for example. What else can I offer, something close at hand and dear to me, as a freely given expression of my devotion to the Lord? I might even find it in an overstocked pantry, offered to those in need, in His name.

Mary took about a pint of pure nard, an expensive perfume;
she poured it on Jesus' feet and wiped his feet with her hair.
And the house was filled with the fragrance of the perfume.
JOHN 12:3

Night Lights

I love night lights. I have one that looks like Marie Antoinette, the light streaming through her large bird's-nest hairstyle. A sleek black-and-white Paris skyline night light graces my guest bathroom. I have tiny, pink track lights in my own bathroom, and under-the-counter lights shine softly in my kitchen. When my daughter moved into her own home, I bought her a night light with bright red poppies, which matched her style.

Night lights are sweet. They say, *Here, don't trip. Don't be afraid.* They give enough light to show you there is nothing to fear, but not so much as to startle you. Night lights are gentle and comforting, and they bring a bit of hope into dark places. When you wake up in the dark, they help orient and reassure. There's a reason toy makers are now inserting night lights into stuffed animals; when little ones squeeze a bear or a baby doll, a bulb goes on, providing comfort and light at the same time.

We believers are night lights, too. We carry within us the greatest light the world has ever known, the one who created light and separated it from the darkness in a physical sense as well as in a spiritual, eternal sense. When we walk into a room, we dispel a little of the mist and fear by our presence and the presence of the one we carry with us (Matthew 5:14–16). We take the hands of those who don't know the way and walk with them, so they don't stumble, so they can see where they can safely walk. Our Light helps orient and reassure both us and those we come into contact with.

You may be a Marie Antoinette style, or you may be a poppy or a skyline or the world's softest teddy bear that everyone wants to love on, and that's okay. Your night light is just right no matter what it looks like.

> *Whoever walks in the dark does not know*
> *where they are going. Believe in the light*
> *while you have the light, so that you may*
> *become children of light.*
> JOHN 12:35–36

Cathedrals

Like many women, I hate mirrors. I avoid them if I can. There's a reason my full-length mirror is hidden behind my always-open bedroom door.

If you've ever visited or lived in Europe (or many other places in our world), you'll remember the many cathedrals. They are skillfully crafted, using the finest stone, wood, marble, and glass. The light filters through windows and arches and casts gorgeous shadows everywhere. Cathedrals are built to be beautiful because they represent where God lives and provide a place to worship Him.

Can you imagine how people would react if someone spat on the floor of a cathedral? Stuck chewed gum on one of the windows? Littered it with candy wrappers? Docents and other worshippers and admirers would be outraged—and rightly so. The culprit would likely be hustled right outside. Everyone would understand this is not how you treat a piece of art, and certainly not God's house and a place of worship.

Scripture tells us that we, God's people, are temples of the Holy Spirit. In fact, we are even more beautiful than those European cathedrals because we are made in His image and created anew in Christ Jesus (Ephesians 2:10). We are His *chosen* home—He lives within us. Therefore, we use our beautiful bodies to work for and worship Him.

Take good care of yourself, not only because you deserve to be treated with honor and dignity but also because your beautiful body is God's home. I'll try not to avoid the mirrors that display the me God loves and chose if you'll do the same.

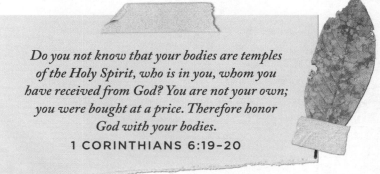

Do you not know that your bodies are temples of the Holy Spirit, who is in you, whom you have received from God? You are not your own; you were bought at a price. Therefore honor God with your bodies.
1 CORINTHIANS 6:19-20

Bared Soles

I bought a small, cheerful plaque a few years back and installed it just outside our front door. It teases, "Please, bare your soles!" Although most guests are okay with this request, some (especially short people like me, who lose precious inches in the process) are uncomfortable at first. Bare feet make us feel vulnerable somehow. Humble. But also, perhaps, more intimate with those we then spend time with inside.

Of course, the reason behind the policy is to protect our home from the mud and muck that shoes inevitably pick up during daily life. Streets are dusted with dirt or iced with dirty snow. Sidewalks are pasted with chewed gum, and the car's carpet (confession time!) is littered with old french fries or coffee straw wrappers.

Even if you don't have a "Shoes off, please" sign, most people have a mat outside their front doors. Very often, it says, "Welcome." Welcome, friends. Welcome, family. Welcome, strangers. It may have a lovely holiday design, or a bright sun painted on it, but it is also usually made with stiff bristles or tough rubber for serious cleaning. Considerate guests scrape their shoes against the mat before entering as a sign of respect for the home.

We read in Scripture that Joshua and Moses were commanded to remove their sandals as a gesture of respect in the presence of God (Joshua 5:15; Exodus 3:5). It's good to realize that God is near and personal, but we sometimes forget to treat Him and His house with appropriate reverence. Sunday mornings can be a rush out the door. Before I leave for church, or at least on the way, I try to take a quiet moment for confession and repentance, scraping off the mud and muck of the week. Taking off my shoes before entering the building. Approaching God's house with humility, respect, and "clean feet." Not criticizing His family, His workers, or the music once I arrive at His house.

I want my guests to feel welcome, but I want them to respect my home, too. How much more should I show respect when God welcomes me into *His* house!

When the LORD saw Moses coming to take a closer look, God called to him from the middle of the bush. . . . "Do not come any closer," the LORD warned. "Take off your sandals, for you are standing on holy ground."
EXODUS 3:4–5 NLT

Kibbles and Bits

One day when my kids were young, I found them crouched, heads down, over our dog's food bowl. The dog stood a fair distance away from them, seemingly as confused as I was. I looked at her, and she looked back; I could almost see her shrug. *Don't ask me. I have no idea what they're doing either.*

Being the calm, collected mom I am, I shouted, "What in the world are you doing?" One child looked up at me and coolly said, "Eating dog food." Perhaps I was a little dull if that was unclear to me. The other said, "The Bible says that dogs eat what falls from the master's table, so we wondered what food that fell from the dog's bowl tasted like." But the looks on their faces indicated that they knew they'd been caught doing something they shouldn't.

I held back a smile. "What does it taste like?" Noses wrinkled. "Dusty graham crackers." I guessed that even if I hadn't interrupted them, the experiment would have soon been over, and they would be rummaging through the pantry for Oreos to cleanse their dusty palates.

So often, we wonder what it tastes like, that which is not intended for us. Is it good? Would we like it? Would it live up to our expectations? Sometimes we even act on the impulse, and then, when caught, we feel guilty. Even though it may taste good for a moment, if it's not for us, it will always leave a bad taste, a sense that we are doing something we shouldn't, and perhaps even more severe consequences (Proverbs 14:12). None of us, even a young child, believe that dog food is good for people. Better to turn away from it, toward the sweet, palate-cleansing property of Oreos—and the sweet Word.

I haven't turned away from your regulations,
for you have taught me well.
How sweet your words taste to me;
they are sweeter than honey.
Your commandments give me understanding;
no wonder I hate every false way of life.
PSALM 119:102–104 NLT

DAY 59
Forced Blooms

I love browsing the floral department in my grocery store in late winter. There are the usual assortments of cacti, cut flowers flown in from the south, and stunning forced-bloom forsythias. The forsythias are noble—long, leggy branches with yellow buds exploding through a thin skin of bark. Eye-catching. Almost prideful.

Once while browsing, I began thinking about those forced blooms, considering which of my outdoor shrubs I could snip from to produce the same effect. But I quickly realized that while cutting branches from my bushes would provide one week's beauty, it would deprive me of the years of enjoyment that the branch could give me if I left it on the shrub. The branch slowly dies once cut and forced to bloom away from its natural environment.

I'd been wrestling with one of my children that week about a personal choice. Nudged to Scripture, I read a familiar passage in Proverbs 22. I'd always taken it to be solely marching orders to train my kids in the faith, but I took a closer look this time. *The way they should go.* That did not necessarily mean the way I thought they should go.

My children are uniquely created; they are not copies of me, or of my husband, or of anyone else. They have singular, God-given destinies; works He created in advance for them alone to do. Their schooling or career choices might not be what I'd thought they would be. They might choose different hairstyles or ink their skin. They may worship at a different kind of church or listen to different music. But if I help them grow in their God-given direction, God will enjoy years—even decades—of them blooming for His glory. God does not want my children to be forced to bloom out of place for the sake of my enjoyment or pride. He wants them to be nurtured to maturity and bloom when and where He'd intended all along.

Start children off on the way they should go,
and even when they are old they
will not turn from it.
PROVERBS 22:6

Dim Bulbs

It is generally understood that to be called a "dim bulb" is not, shall we say, the highest praise. And yet there are times when a dim bulb is precisely what is called for.

I like the under-cabinet lighting in my kitchen; it lends a lovely ambiance to the room. I like the faint light that illuminates my stairway. It's not lit up like a runway, but it's bright enough so that no one will trip. Every woman of a certain age knows that candlelight is more becoming than the bright bulbs in her makeup mirror. And low-watt night lights are just perfect for getting around in the dark.

God's Word illuminates every aspect of our lives. We understand that Scripture is profitable for teaching, correcting, rebuking, and training. We know it sheds light on our paths and that it can help others. The problem is, there may be times when we who are further along the path may be too eager to shine a spotlight of truth on others who are less mature in the faith (Romans 15:1–2).

Our ability to tolerate the brighter light of faith increases over time. Others, younger in their faith or wounded or more vulnerable, may need the soft radiance of a muted light, to begin with. We needn't, for example, point out every possible sin to avoid or offer suggestions for a dozen new spiritual disciplines to begin at once. Discipleship is a patient process (Galatians 6:2). Sanctification is a gentle art. Gradually, over time, that dimmer switch can be turned up.

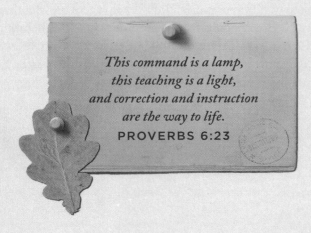

This command is a lamp,
this teaching is a light,
and correction and instruction
are the way to life.
PROVERBS 6:23

Roaring Lions

My dog hides. My daughter's cat hides. If the pets across the street could hear and see it, they would hide, too.

The vacuum cleaner is on.

I only have to open the closet where the beast is caged, and my dog runs for the hills. If the stairs are blocked, she'll jump up onto the fireplace hearth, the wimp. But is she a wimp? The machine is about six times her size and is loud even to me, never mind to delicate canine ears. The machine seems to follow her around the house, or at least makes a sweep through every room (when I have time), seeming to leave no area as a sanctuary. When I shut it down, and silence ensues, I can see my dog relax and return to her perch on the back of the couch, fearful no longer—till the next time, anyway.

Still, doesn't she know that, as fearsome and loud as the beast is, I am in control of it? I, her trusted and beloved pet parent? Have I ever once let it eat her? Harm her? Have I chased her with it on purpose? Of course not. She should trust me; she should know that even though it prowls the grounds from time to time, it is never out of my control, as scary as it may seem. I can quickly turn it off and pull the plug, although I let it roar from time to time for purposes that only I can understand.

Luke 22:31 shows us that Satan had to ask God if he could sift the disciple Peter as he would wheat. And not only Peter but "all of you," that is, the disciples. We, too, are Jesus's disciples, and God sometimes allows us to be sifted for purposes only He understands. He also enables us to be strong.

Thank you, Father, that although Satan sifts, roars, and prowls, you are still in control. I am in your hands—hands that have never done me wrong.

Be alert and of sober mind. Your enemy
the devil prowls around like a roaring lion
looking for someone to devour.
1 PETER 5:8

Times and Seasons

Late autumn is a lovely time to take a walk; I can see things in fall's stark beauty that I can't see at any other time.

Once, while walking through the woods, I could see a "widow maker," a tree that had fallen and was resting, unstable, against another thin tree. I knew that when it fell the rest of the way, it would do so quickly and take down whatever or whoever was in its path.

After the leaves had all fallen from the Japanese maples in my backyard, I spotted an elaborate bird's nest in the upper branches. I had seen its residents but had not seen where they lived . . . till then.

I like to prune my shrubs and trees in late autumn because without the cover of leaves, I can clearly see where they need clipping to take on the shape I'd like them to have.

The starkness of the dormant season reveals things to me that I can't see in the dense lushness of spring and summer.

Although I don't like undergoing dormant seasons in my own life when I wonder if God still loves me or has a purpose or plan for me, I know that those quiet seasons allow me to make assessments and adjustments where needed. Seasons are entirely within God's control, both on earth and in my life. He rearranges as He sees fit, and it's always for His glory—and my good. His changes are always beneficial: remove the fallen, dangerous tree; show me life where I'd not seen it before; help shape me in the way we both know is best. I have come to love our quiet seasons.

He changes times and seasons;
he deposes kings and raises up others.
He gives wisdom to the wise
and knowledge to the discerning.
He reveals deep and hidden things;
he knows what lies in darkness,
and light dwells with him.
DANIEL 2:21-22

DAY 63
Soft Wax

One day, I sat at the kitchen table, surrounded by bits of ephemera and photos from our family trip to London. I'd set aside the afternoon to scrapbook the pieces so we'd be able to page through them later.

I came across the ticket stub for Madame Tussauds. Marie Tussaud began her illustrious career making wax portraits just before and during the French Revolution. Afterward, she made her way to Great Britain, where she continued to make life-sized wax figures of the rich and famous. Wax is cheaper and easier to work with than metal or stone. It can be colored and molded and altered, if need be, over time. It doesn't break as clay does but molds perfectly and conforms exactly to the shape it is pressed into. That's why, when you visit the museum, the celebrities look so lifelike. We had our pictures taken with "The Beatles" at the museum. And with "the Queen."

Although not celebrities, we, too, are to be waxlike. Soft and pliable in the hand of the One who made us, who conforms us to His pattern (Isaiah 64:8). From our perspective, each new day seems to bring an unexpected twist—good or bad—or a situation we had not anticipated. God saw all this coming (Hebrews 4:13) and uses our circumstances to mold and shape us. According to Scripture, He does this by conforming us, over time, to the image of His Son.

Be soft and pliable. He who models you loves you.

Those God foreknew he also predestined to
be conformed to the image of his Son, that
he might be the firstborn among many
brothers and sisters.
ROMANS 8:29

I Am Still Alive

The previous owners of one of our houses were people who loved decorating but hated gardening. So when we went to overhaul the backyard, we pulled out many plants that had become diseased or had died from neglect. Against the back fence, though, I found one long, straggly rose, twining herself to a small piece of careworn lattice.

She'd been planted in the wrong place entirely. There was very little natural sunlight, and what was there was up high, so she'd been forced to push her vine up tall to reach it. The soil had not been amended, so it was thin and nutrient poor. Water came only when the skies provided it, not through drip or hose. Her leaves showed signs of bite marks. But the most remarkable thing about this rose was not all the hardships she had endured. It was her color and her perfume.

Her bloom was a pale lilac, ethereal, the color of the clouds at twilight. Her scent was distilled sweetness, ladylike, sugar and spice, and everything nice. Despite the conditions in which she was forced to live, she had not only survived; she'd thrived.

Although she did not seem to fit into my garden plan, I could not cut her down. She seemed to say, *In spite of it all, I am still alive.*

So I kept her and planned my garden around her instead. More valuable to me than a perfect scheme was the lesson she brought, one I knew I had needed in the past and would no doubt need again. No matter where and how we're planted or how thin the soil seems, God will enable His roses to thrive.

*Those who trust in their
riches will fall,
but the righteous will
thrive like a green leaf.*
PROVERBS 11:28

That Wretched Grass

I had a dry triangle of land between my garage and a walking path. It was in the hot sun, and it was a difficult place to water. I thought about putting rock in there and calling it good, but then I remembered how much I liked a friend's sedum, also called stonecrop. Perfect! Stonecrop wants to be hot, dry, and neglected. Why can't all of my plants be so easy?

So I planted mats of sedum there—kind of like laying down a piece of carpet, only plants. A couple of months later, willowy strands of grass poked their way up through the sedum mat. Pulling them out at the roots also pulled out the sedum, the very plants I wanted to keep. *I should have rocked this over*, I thought, exasperated. But no, I really loved the sedum. I decided that I'd just give the grass a haircut and hope the sedum got strong enough to crowd out the weeds.

It did!

Jesus told a parable about a farmer who planted good seed in his fields (Matthew 13:24–30). While his workers were sleeping, an enemy came in and sowed weeds among the farmer's good crops. They grew up together, close, weed and plant. If the farmer's workers had pulled out the weeds while the good plants were still young, the good plants might have been pulled out as well.

It's easy for me to have strong opinions about which people are "good plants" and which are "weeds." And sometimes I wonder why God allows clearly evil people to survive and sometimes even appear to thrive. Perhaps the answer is in Jesus's parable and the garden of sedum.

"An enemy has done this!" the farmer exclaimed. "Should we pull out the weeds?" they asked. "No," he replied, "you'll uproot the wheat if you do. Let both grow together until the harvest. Then I will tell the harvesters to sort out the weeds."

MATTHEW 13:28-30 NLT

Lining Things Up

Our front garden includes a long stretch that faces the street and is in full view of everyone. Because of that, it makes the first statement about our home. It was a lovely place to put hedges and shrubs, but we wanted to ensure that everything was placed exactly right because it was so visible.

We capped off the ends with barberries (deer hate them) and then took a tape measure and marked off eight-foot sections in between them for all the other shrubs. A little squirt of chalk powder helped us remember where to plant each one, and when we had finished, it was exactly as we had hoped and planned.

God takes the long view, too, especially with something so important to Him and the world as His plan for the redemption of humanity through Jesus. He carefully lined things up. Starting with Adam and Eve, we can see God's faithfulness—although sin had been introduced, a blood sacrifice was made to atone for it. In Genesis 22, Abraham was asked to sacrifice his son Isaac, but when Isaac spoke up, noting that the fire and the wood were ready, but asked where the lamb for the burnt offering was, Abraham responded prophetically, "God, he himself, will provide the lamb," foreshadowing the death of Jesus. Leviticus 17 speaks of the blood sacrifice required for atonement. And John the Baptist speaks of Jesus as the Lamb who came to take away the sins of the world, restoring our relationship with the Father (John 1:29).

God laid out all the events, in line, in the correct order, and at the right time so we can see how it all relates. He has always required sacrifice to cover sin; He is the same yesterday, today, and tomorrow. But He has also always provided that sacrifice himself, sparing not even His own Son in His desire to restore His relationship with you and me.

God—who does not lie—promised them [eternal
life] before the world began. And now at just the
right time he has revealed this message.
TITUS 1:2-3 NLT

Singleness

The savvy home decorator knows to group things in odd numbers. An even number of objects, arranged symmetrically, is too predictable to please the eye. But one candle, surrounded by three framed pictures, in a room with five pieces of furniture, creates interest and natural elegance.

Odd numbers may be acceptable in decorating, but it seems like things are designed for two in real life, especially if you are single. Dinner for two at a nice restaurant. Buy-one-get-one-free deals for entertainment options. Driver and passenger. Double beds. It can be very lonely to be single in a world that seems to be designed for couples.

Sometimes the Lord cures that loneliness with the provision of a mate. Sometimes He satisfies it with friends and family or fulfilling activities. For some singles, He simply removes the desire for romantic companionship. But even so, many single people wish that they weren't.

There are no easy answers that aren't simplistic or perhaps even offensive. There is a biblical response, however. We, all of us believers, have an eternal bridegroom, in Jesus Christ (John 3:29). Christ, too, understands what it is like to be unmarried in a society in which couples are the norm. His calling included singleness, single beds, and loneliness.

He will not call any of us to a place where He will not accompany us and equip us. And He will never leave us nor forsake us.

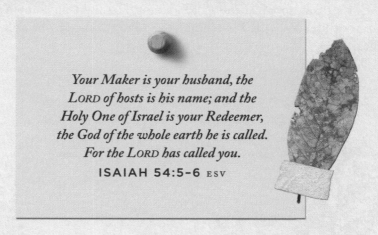

Your Maker is your husband, the LORD of hosts is his name; and the Holy One of Israel is your Redeemer, the God of the whole earth he is called. For the LORD has called you.

ISAIAH 54:5-6 ESV

DAY 68
Sunshine Smudges

After a long, dark winter, one of the best things about spring is the sunshine that becomes more plentiful. One room I spend a lot of time in is my kitchen, which has lovely windows that let in that glorious sunlight. I love it for the cheer it brings, but there's something I definitely begin to notice in that bright glow—the beams do more than spread happiness. They also reveal a winter's worth of dust, dirt, smudges, and smears on my cabinet fronts, windows, and appliances. I hadn't seen the faint smears in the winter gloom.

When the Lord draws near to us and gently whispers or convicts us about something wrong in our lives, He's bringing light to an area that He wants us to see afresh (John 8:12). It might be a habit that needs to be cleaned away, like overspending. Perhaps it's a tendency toward thoughtless action that smudges the pure beauty of our hearts, like laziness, self-pity, or being quick to anger. Instead, He is patient, slow to anger, and filled with loving-kindness (Numbers 14:18; Psalm 103:8), and patient toward us and wishes for us to repent (2 Peter 3:9). As we draw near to Him to become clean again, He draws near to us (James 4:8).

The time to clean things up is as soon as we can see that it needs to be done. His bright light isn't shining on me to condemn; it's to bring that fresh, new feeling I get once I wipe down the cupboard and the fridge, ready for spring days ahead.

Can you, too, feel the Lord shining His light on some dark places in your life? What is He telling you? Quiet yourself—be still. Can you hear Him?

I could ask the darkness to hide me
and the light around me to become night—
but even in darkness I cannot hide from you.
To you the night shines as bright as day.
Darkness and light are the same to you.
PSALM 139:11-12 NLT

DAY 69
Sowing Seeds

S ome of the plants I'd most like to grow, like tomatoes, don't grow easily in my cool corner of the country. I've tried tucking little seeds into tiny, thimble-sized planting pots, hoping and praying they would sprout. Despite my motherly attention, most of them didn't. When they died, it hurt.

Sometimes the seeds sprout only to stop growing at one or two inches, which was so disappointing. Hope allowed to endure, only to be quickly extinguished, can be more painful than no hope at all. A couple of times, I've planted tomatoes that made it to fruit—unripe fruit, which I desperately wanted to redeem, wishing that my efforts had not been in vain. I now understand the previously untested charms of fried green tomato sandwiches!

In some ways, allowing ourselves to hope is like planting vegetable seeds. We want something to happen, come about, and bear goodness in our own life or in the life of someone we love. So we work toward it, pray about it, ask God for it, and ask others to pray, too. But just as with planting, there is an inherent risk of disappointment in hope. Faithfully planting seeds into the lives of others without a guarantee of return makes us vulnerable. It opens us up to the possibility of loss and discouragement when what is wished for fails to sprout, dies young, or bears unripe fruit.

Sometimes, though, the plants *do* grow. My neighbor prayed over his plants, to little avail. Then he got smart in our wet and cool climate and bought a mini hothouse. Into many tiny pots on rows over wooden shelves, he sowed tomatoes. Later that summer, he had baskets of warm, ripe reds, so many that he'd bless a particular neighbor each week with a basket of his overflow!

The apostle Paul tells us that love always hopes (1 Corinthians 13:7). Because of Christ, who first loved us (1 John 4:19), we can expect in confidence that the seeds meant to sprout will. Sow into your own life and the lives of others a variety of hopes—widely, generously, without fear— then combine those hopes with wise actions. Some seeds will sprout, and some will not.

If you never plant a seed, you're never disappointed, but you never have the satisfaction of eating your own delicious, homegrown, Big Boy tomato, either.

Remember this—a farmer who plants only a few seeds will get a small crop. But the one who plants generously will get a generous crop.

2 CORINTHIANS 9:6 NLT

Tea for Two

I have a good listener friend, which is commendable (Proverbs 1:5). Now, everyone wants a friend who is a good listener, not so much the one who is a good talker. (Note to self: remember this.) My friend has a compassionate heart, she never interrupts, and when it's her turn to speak, she does so with love and grace as well as sound advice. Perhaps Solomon had someone like her in mind when he wrote, "A word fitly spoken is like apples of gold in a setting of silver" (Proverbs 25:11 ESV).

The problem is, by the time people are done speaking their piece and receiving her counsel, they feel better, but she feels drained. It's not as often that someone listens to *her* or understands the time alone that she requires to dispense those silver-set apples.

One year for her birthday, I bought her two teacups—British, as her reading pleasures lean that way. The idea was that when she sat down with her friends—talking with them, listening and confiding, taking in and offering—she needed to have her cup filled up as much as she needed to fill the cups of others. She and her friend should drain their cups and fill their hearts at equal rates. If her cup was empty—from listening and not talking—before her friend's was, they could both take polite notice without calling one another out.

Our communication patterns are not easy to break, whether we're talker friends or listener friends. A listener friend needs to learn to be brave, vulnerable, and willing to speak up more often: if you want to be heard, you have to say something. And a talker friend needs to learn to sit back and use her mouth for sipping her tea while her ears are engaged.

It's beautiful to pour into others, whether a delightful Earl Grey or a word given in season. Just make sure that you let others do the talking if you're the talker, and let others care for you, too, if you're the listener. Working together, sharing strengths, arms, hearts, and love—and tea— benefits both of you.

Two are better than one,
because they have a good return for their labor:
If either of them falls down,
one can help the other up.
ECCLESIASTES 4:9–10

Would Anyone Guess a Christian Lives Here?

One afternoon my husband and I walked room to room looking for lightbulbs and smoke detector batteries that needed to be replaced.

We walked from the French country–inspired living room to the library with lots of throw blankets and pillows, to the kitchen with pink-and-black granite, to the powder room with a lavender night light. I sensed more than heard the grumbling. "What?" I asked him.

"Would anyone even know a man lives in this place?" he groused. I laughed and pointed out the man cave, the garage, and the lawn. He nodded, kind of convinced.

He'd made a point, though. Although we're not to judge by appearance, we do look at people and their environs to get a sense of what they are about. Do they treat people in private the same as in public, or are they hypocrites? Do they rail against "sins" that are not forbidden but which may be more a matter of personal taste, and at the same time defend the exercise of free will? What's on their movie list? What kinds of books do they have in their homes? Music on their playlists? Do they never have enough money for charity but plenty for travel?

This isn't meant to be a defense for legalism nor an excuse to point out the speck in our brother's eye (Matthew 7:5). In fact, by showing that we can enjoy freedom in Christ, we might be showing people a different view of Christianity than the restricted legalism they're expecting. Still, we must always be aware that those around us will be learning by observation not only about us but about our faith—and that includes the freedom we enjoy as well. Do your home and your life reflect your heart for Christ?

Whatever you have learned or received or heard
from me, or seen in me—put it into practice.
And the God of peace will be with you.
PHILIPPIANS 4:9

Washing Whites

I admire homemakers who have sorting baskets in their laundry rooms—one for whites, one for colors, one for delicates. As for me, the most incredible thing I discovered on my new washing machine was the setting for "Mixed Loads." I'm usually too busy (lazy? hurried?) to use anything else.

The problem, of course, is that some garments really do need to be set aside. The sleeves on men's dress shirts can shrink if washed in hot water or dried for too long. (Do not ask me how I know this!) A too-energetic agitator can shred delicates. And dark colors, especially reds, can bleed.

It's easy to end up with pink whites—T-shirts, towels, or socks—as a result of overlooking a new red something thrown into the wash with them. Then drastic measures are required to avert replacing said garments. Removing the offensive red piece and then rewashing the pinks with bleach usually does the trick. Everything returns to snowy white, as it should be.

Like a launderer's detergent, God convicts us even when we are too lazy or busy to pay attention and have let sin bleed into our lives. Sometimes I forget that sin taints everything I do if left unaddressed. God doesn't judge me when I humbly bring my sin-stained efforts to Him. He takes them from me, bleaches them with His holiness, and makes me pure again. The cost? Inestimable. But Jesus willingly paid it all, and remembering that encourages me to take great care of all He has entrusted to me.

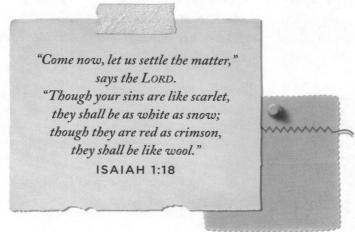

"Come now, let us settle the matter,"
says the LORD.
"Though your sins are like scarlet,
they shall be as white as snow;
though they are red as crimson,
they shall be like wool."

ISAIAH 1:18

For the Love of a Sparrow

I went out one late-spring morning to water the geraniums in my window box. As I moved the watering wand inside the box, a bird flew out at me—nearly colliding with my nose. I came closer but saw nothing. Then I spotted it—a little nest with four oval eggs. I was a landlord! My geranium box had tenants! I asked my neighbors about the birds and learned the new residents were juncos, a kind of sparrow.

I had never had nests built so close to my house, on "land" that I was responsible for instead of in the trees edging the lawn. What should I do next? I turned to my social media accounts to ask my friends. Do I water? If I do, will the birds or their nest be harmed? But if I don't, will the plants die and expose my young bird family to danger? I knew there were aggressive blue jays and crows nearby.

Within minutes I had dozens of comments: suggestions on how to water the plant without harming the birds, ways to deadhead the flowers without cutting back the cover, and requests to share the news when the birdies were born.

It was so heartwarming. These were only birds, after all. But people cared, and they were eager to help me attend to them. I could only imagine what wonderful assistance and love these dear people would offer if I had asked for help for a child!

The lesson was not lost on me. I cared deeply for those sparrows; I felt responsible to protect them. But my affection for them was nothing compared to my affection for my children, for whom I would lay down my life. God nudged me. I grinned. *Yeah, I get it, God. Thank you—really. Thank you.*

Are not two sparrows sold for a penny?
Yet not one of them will fall to the ground
outside your Father's care. And even the
very hairs of your head are all numbered.
So don't be afraid; you are worth more
than many sparrows.
MATTHEW 10:29-31

Free to Fly

*Run, John, run,
the law commands,
But gives us neither feet
nor hands.
Far better news
the gospel brings:
It bids us fly
and gives us wings.*

Attributed to John Bunyan

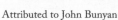

In our geranium flower-box "hotel" that summer, the resident junco family made a featherweight straw nest and promptly laid little eggs in it. Within just a few short weeks (wherein I neither watered nor deadheaded), the birds hatched, received food, and were urged out of the nest and into the nearby trees. It seemed that Mom and Dad taught them to fly almost as soon as they emerged from their shells. I looked it up: the little chirpers leave the nest about two weeks after hatching.

The birds were not destined to stay flightless within the confines of a nest, no matter how safe and comfortable. The truth is, the nest wouldn't be very comfortable for six grown birds. They needed the freedom to do what they were created to do—fly.

Likewise, we believers are not meant to be confined to faith by rules, safe as it sometimes may seem. The Old Testament law provided safe boundaries for God's people, but Jesus fulfilled the law for us. We no longer have to worry that we don't measure up; that we haven't followed all the rules; or that our sacrifice, work, and offerings will be rejected. We are right with God and need not perform to be acceptable. We can always return to His sheltering wing, but we are also free to fly.

*If the old way, which brings condemnation,
was glorious, how much more glorious is the
new way, which makes us right with God!*
2 CORINTHIANS 3:9 NLT

Empty Nests

So soon, too soon, it was time for our little junco family to leave the nest. Mama and Papa bird had taught their young ones to fly, and they were twittering happily in the backyard trees. One morning I looked in my geranium boxes and found that the nest was empty.

That resonated with me. My children have flown away from the nest, moving forward into their own lives even while inextricably connected to mine. I was happy for them to be reaching forward into the joyful autonomy of adulthood while feeling, I admit, a little at odds about my new role in their lives and in the world in general. Being a hands-on mom had been such a big part of my daily life for so long. It is no more.

I noticed that the junco parents had completely cleaned out the nest after their young had flown away. And they did not nest in that place again; they, too, had moved on. Perhaps there is a lesson there. Maybe you don't have children, or your children are still young. You may be widowed or divorced or just lost your job or house. We each have seasons wherein an era we love comes to a close. We move to a different stage of life—maybe willingly, perhaps unwillingly. You might be flailing a little, as I was, struggling to discover a new purpose and direction, wondering if the old fits in somehow while trying to welcome the new.

Had the parent birds remained in that empty nest, it would have felt odd. But they'd flown on, too, to other areas, other trees. It is a great big world, after all, and there are new things to experience and explore even as seasons march on, fresh things in life to discover and enjoy. The nest may be empty, but life is full for the junco birds and maybe for me, too, in the here and now.

There's an opportune time to do things, a
right time for everything on the earth:
. . . a time to hold on and another to let go.
ECCLESIASTES 3:1, 6 MSG

DAY 76
Yellow Rose of Texas

I could never plant roses in our front yard because the neighborhood deer looked at them the way you and I might look at a luscious piece of whipped cream–topped pound cake. The roses would be chewed up and gone in an hour. But there was one tiny, empty corner in my fenced backyard, a spot that received lots of sun. Since I had only one small space suitable for roses, I had to carefully consider which type to plant. It wasn't a difficult decision at all. I'd plant the yellow roses of Texas.

One of my best, dearest friends passed away from cancer some years ago. She'd often talked of the flowers of Texas, the bluebonnets, and the roses. When she died, some mutual friends sent a bouquet of yellow roses to me, a touching gesture that I have never forgotten. One of those blossoms is pressed inside my Bible.

As I dug the hole before planting, I thought about my friend. She'd left behind two boys—boys who would not have their mother to guide and comfort them. As a mom, I wanted to always be around to advise and encourage, as I sometimes feel only a mother can. My friend died knowing that she could no longer mother her kids, but she had firm faith that the Lord himself would guide and guard her children. And He has.

Although I will see her again someday, I am still here on this earth, and I realize that I can hand my ever-present concerns for my children and grandchildren into God's hands right now; my death is not required, first, to hand over to Him in principle what He's always held in fact. He can care for them when I'm not here and while I *am* here, too. I need not worry. He is faithful.

I am grateful for my dear friend, my Yellow Rose of Texas, who still teaches me.

Know therefore that the Lord your God is God;
he is the faithful God, keeping his covenant of
love to a thousand generations of those who love
him and keep his commandments.
DEUTERONOMY 7:9

Level Ground

One of the most onerous jobs when installing hardscaping—the firm, permanent landscape features such as rock beds, fountains, and fences—is leveling the ground. It's not as simple as just scraping the land and eyeballing it. One must carefully consider the slope of the ground, measure precisely, and recruit several sets of eyes because what looks fine to one person can, in actuality, be way off. Perspective is needed.

All people are born into a world with unlevel playing fields. Some are born rich, some poor. Some are born into groups of people who suffer unjust discrimination, and others into more protected segments of society. Some are born into nations that protect their freedoms; others are persecuted. Some are born into families that nurture and cherish them, and some into families that abuse. There is little that is truly fair or just here on earth. Yet our souls cry out for justice because we are made in God's image, and He is perfectly just.

If God is just, why is there so much that is unjust in the here and now? When Jesus came to earth, His people were expecting a Messiah who would be an earthly king, one who would take power and avenge them then and there. Instead, Jesus came gently on a donkey, which disappointed them but fulfilled the prophecy in a way they didn't understand. When Christ returns, He will come in power and strength and set things right. They will remain right for all eternity.

Though born into a variety of circumstances, all of us are equal brothers and sisters in Christ. No one is better, more valuable, more protected, or more cherished. We're each precious in the sight of our Savior. He will put right any inequities in our current situations . . . in His time. To live the full and rich life He's given us and not be swayed by those unlevel playing fields, we must understand He has a long game and adopt His perspective.

There is neither Jew nor Gentile, neither
slave nor free, nor is there male and
female, for you are all one in Christ Jesus.
GALATIANS 3:28

Pay It Forward

I browsed the home supply store one day, looking for some film that I could apply to windows in our house in rooms that needed a little bit of privacy. I didn't want to block the light entirely (in one room, it was the only window!), and I wanted it to look pretty. A cut-to-fit scroll of film designed to look like stained glass fit the bill.

When I got home, my straightedge and I headed upstairs to affix my purchase to the window, which took a speedy fifteen minutes. I laughed at that, recalling the beautiful, breathtaking stained glass windows I had seen in a thirteenth-century cathedral in France just a few years before. The docent leading the tour told us that the windows were many years in the making; it might take two, three, or even four generations of artisans to finish a single window. One artisan may have designed the window but never seen it under construction. Another may have begun the work but seen only bits and pieces of the final product. Only the last craftsman would see the project completed. Those who came before him had to trust that the future workers would carry their vision forward. They couldn't have been working for the accolades of the worshippers; they'd never see them. They had to work for the praise of the Worshipped alone.

Many "projects" we undertake will bear fruit that we will never see. Often we do what we feel led to do, but we do not see it succeed. We plant seeds that do not seem to sprout. We pour ourselves into the lives of those who don't turn themselves around. If we keep our eyes on circumstantial affirmation, we're bound to be disappointed. But if we keep our eyes on the Worshipped alone, we work knowing that we'll reap a generous reward.

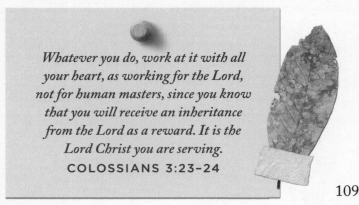

Whatever you do, work at it with all your heart, as working for the Lord, not for human masters, since you know that you will receive an inheritance from the Lord as a reward. It is the Lord Christ you are serving.
COLOSSIANS 3:23–24

DAY 79
Seedlings

Spring is a season for planting. While the ground is still hard, we take tools and loosen it up some, breaking big clumps of dirt into soft mounds of black and brown soil. Once it's softened, we place a seed in it or a tiny plant that needs to take root. We know that even though it doesn't look like much at that point, each has the potential to grow into something beautiful.

Too little water, and the seed or plant dies. Too much rain, and the water rolls away, down into the grass or onto the sidewalk. Or maybe it lifts the plant out of its new bed or washes the seed away, only to dry up and die, so close to home.

Jesus is living water for our souls; our spirits cannot live without Him (John 4:14). Meditating on God's Word allows us to be well-watered and live wonderful lives (Psalm 1:2–3), and, of course, we want that for others. When we've known Jesus for a while, we want to speak truth with our friends who don't yet know Christ or are new to the faith. And that's terrific! But if we try to share too much at once, their minds wander as ours once did, and the good that it might do doesn't happen (Acts 15:13–15, 19); the extra "water" just rolls down the sidewalk. Or maybe the flow of biblical truth is so overwhelming that it lifts them out of the flower bed altogether, and Scripture becomes a lecture, turning them off to the truth.

Your friends are lovely seedlings developing into beautiful flowers, and you are an amazing friend to share your water. Just make sure you are watering with measured portions, allowing time for God's truth to be absorbed—slow but steady growth is best (Acts 8:30–31, 34–35). Then watch as, over time, the Gardener grows your friends into sturdy plants, too!

Such things were written in the Scriptures
long ago to teach us. And the Scriptures
give us hope and encouragement as we wait
patiently for God's promises to be fulfilled.
ROMANS 15:4 NLT

Habits

I'd planted a flower bed right before some significant work and personal deadlines approached. *At least the plants are in,* I reassured myself. *I can leave them alone for a while.*

But when some time had passed, and I returned to my garden, I found that weeds had commandeered my bed. They'd settled in with the plants, stealing my plants' food. The weeds began to crowd the flowers; they grew tall, shading my own blossoms so they couldn't get the sun they needed.

It took weeks to get all of those weeds out because they'd become tough and persistent. The flower bed had become dominated by what was wrong instead of what was right. The weeds were beginning to damage the good plants (1 Corinthians 15:33). Had I kept on top of those weeds, I could have stopped them before things had gotten so out of hand.

That's what I did after that experience. I also promised myself to plant fewer flower beds!

If I attend to the things I know are good for me—body, mind, and spirit—I'm rooted and built up in health and strength. But when I get lazy and let my physical health slide to indulge in bad habits, or my mental health slide to indulge in lazy entertainment, or my spiritual health slide because I'm willing to let other things crowd out what's valuable, I'm vulnerable to philosophies contrary to my faith.

Plucking out a weed or two when they're small and few is so much easier than eradicating them after they have taken over the entire bed.

Just as you received Christ Jesus as Lord, continue to live your lives in Him, rooted and built up in Him, strengthened in the faith as you were taught, and overflowing with thankfulness.

See to it that no one takes you captive
through hollow and deceptive philosophy,
which depends on human tradition and
the elemental spiritual forces of this world
rather than on Christ.
COLOSSIANS 2:8

DAY 81
Stuffed Armoires

I'd made a really good friend online; we bonded over our shared love of reading and our newly launched writing careers. Soon we were emailing every day, sharing more than our writing. We shared our prayer requests, financial concerns, health issues, and worries about our families. We confessed our sins to each other (James 5:16) and held each other accountable.

One spring, she and I were both freshening up our homes and decided to send pictures to each other via email since we didn't live close enough to visit. So after cleaning up my house, I went from room to room, snapping photos from the best angles. Then I sent them to her. Within a day or so, she responded.

"Beautiful house," she said. "But it's so . . . neat. Where's all your stuff?"

I laughed at that. I knew what she meant. Magazines, dog-grooming brushes, socks taken off before a nap the day before, TV remotes . . . I had discovered the magic of armoires and placed one in almost every room. When I wanted the room to look pulled together and neat, without anything out of place, I'd pile all the clutter in the armoire. It wasn't long before it all migrated out again, though.

Do you pile all of your "stuff" in armoires, hidden from everyone and anyone who can help? It was great to have that comment come from a friend with whom I could be honest, one who trusted me with honesty about the details of her life in return (1 Thessalonians 5:11). I can let it all hang out with those I trust, confess my faults, and ask for help. It's good to have friends who don't mind your stuff.

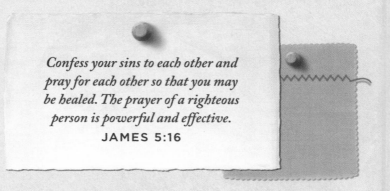

Confess your sins to each other and pray for each other so that you may be healed. The prayer of a righteous person is powerful and effective.

JAMES 5:16

Ministry of a Mess

There was a pile of toys on the floor—I'd stepped on several building blocks and let out a loud cry of pain. The toddler had taken a five-hundred-count box of tissues and pulled them out, one by one. Apparently, no one had let the dog out. The shoes were reproducing themselves in the corner. Why is it that dirty clothes seem to generate spontaneously?

We'd had Bible study here the night before, and I hadn't gotten to the dishes yet. My home office was stacked with files and books that looked like multiple Leaning Towers of Pisa.

I like a clean house; I really do. I like my office tidy, too. But as it has been said many times by many people, there are only so many hours in a day. So I had to make some choices. Which was more important: comforting a child who'd been bullied or throwing away the rotting lettuce in my refrigerator? Taking a call from a friend whose mother had been diagnosed with terminal cancer or balancing the checkbook? In times like these, I thought of Deuteronomy 6:7 and recognized the importance of "being" there instead of doing the tasks. On some rare days, I'm caught up, but mostly, I'm not. And that's okay.

A messy desk is a sign of a productive mind. A kitchen with dirty dishes is being used. Toys all over the room mean kids are playing. Books splayed about on every surface prove we're reading and learning. A hug from my kid means that she believes she's going to recover.

Scripture tells us that a barn in disarray means that working animals are present; things are happening there. Without the oxen, nothing gets done. At the end of the day, or the week, or our lives, no one will remember how clean (or not) our houses were, but they'll remember and feel, deep down, how we loved and cared for them there.

Without oxen a stable stays clean,
but you need a strong ox for a large harvest.
PROVERBS 14:4 NLT

Read the Directions

I couldn't figure out how the box for such a large piece of furniture could comfortably fit inside the back of our car, but it did! I happily made my way home, envisioning the television and books arranged on the new piece, thinking and talking about how it would enhance our lives. Once home, I understood how the box had fit into the car. When it was opened, dozens of pieces fell out, along with a hefty tome labeled "Assembly Instructions."

Now, I'm the person who scrolls all the way through the dozen pages of digital agreements for apps and websites, not reading, just clicking on "I Agree." So I was not going to waste an hour reading directions when putting part AA into part ZZ with screw HH and bolt 253 couldn't be that hard! An hour later, the piece was assembled. Two hours later, it wobbled and nearly collapsed, almost taking the TV with it.

I went back to the instructions. Surprising things can be found when one reads the directions. Humbled, I reassembled the piece of furniture in the proper order, thankful that I had not done any lasting damage.

Surprising things, too, can be found when we read sections of the Bible that we thought we knew. I find myself saying, much too often, "I know the Bible says ____, but I can't remember where." Or, "Memorization is my worst discipline." Or, "I remember it's something like . . ." Unfortunately, too often, when I take the time to look up the exact verse, I realize I've forgotten some crucial points. I've learned that I'd better not quote the Sandra Paraphrase because it's close enough to sound good but far enough off to do some real damage.

Read the instructions, and follow them closely, I tell myself. The structural integrity of the Word is much more important than the security of the TV.

Do your best to present yourself to God
as one approved, a worker who does not
need to be ashamed and who correctly
handles the word of truth.
2 TIMOTHY 2:15

Soft Chairs

My husband and I were visiting our new friends' house for the first time to attend a small group meeting. After some shuffling around, we all went to sit in their family room. Members made their way to the couches, the love seat, and the kitchen chairs brought in for the occasion. No one sat in the recliner, though, because, as my husband said, "No one sits in another man's chair."

At our house, we each have our special place. My husband has his chair, and no one else sits in it except the dog—if she can get away with it. Mostly she prefers any blanket pulled to the floor. My daughter is petite and loves the love seat, especially now that she's married. Our son likes the soft couch in the man cave. And I like the little chair in a reading nook, complete with a warm blanket and a small table for my books and Bibles.

It's where I go when everyone else has left the house, a place of quiet and peace, where I meet with God. I didn't always have a special place to meet with Him because I know He is with me everywhere. But when I set aside a place and made it cozy and left a Bible there, it beckoned to me, as Jesus did with His disciples (Luke 6:31), to come away more often. And as I did, I drew closer to God and Him to me.

We spend so much of our time helping others and providing comfort. We love, we soothe, and we give up what we want or need to meet the wants or needs of another. And for the most part, that's fulfilling. But Scripture encourages us to love others *as we love ourselves*, which suggests we need to do loving things for ourselves as well. So find a place just for you, a place where you can read, rest, and get away to meet with God. You deserve that tender care, too.

Come near to God and he will come near to you.
JAMES 4:8

Upgrading My Gratitude

You've probably read the Ten Commandments, even though it may have been a while. I reviewed them again recently, and I was feeling pretty smug. In no way do I covet my neighbor's donkey or ox. I am not aware that any of my friends have a servant for me to covet, though I definitely grow a little wistful when I hear of people who have weekly housekeeping service. However, I admit to one area of covetousness.

I covet houses.

And the world is ready to help me do just that! On television, there is show after show of remodeling, redoing, or reworking; buying, bidding, or selling. I sometimes watch them, lusting for the houses I'll never have, mouth agape at the realization that people have that kind of cash to drop on decorating.

Then there are the websites that send me an alert when one of my neighbors is selling a house. Am I interested? You bet I am. There are times (head hangs here) I scroll through to see what the interiors of their homes look like and what upgrades they've made. *I'm collecting ideas*, I tell myself. But I envy. I really do, especially when I have to spend money on a broken water heater instead of replacing the threadbare carpet.

It's easy for me to rationalize that lusting after a house isn't as bad as lusting after my neighbor's husband. But the tenth commandment doesn't distinguish between the two. They both involve desiring and lusting for what does not belong to me. Lust of any kind makes us discontent with what and whom we've been given . . . or not given. It makes us envious, which leads us, like Eve, to the temptation (Genesis 3:1) of questioning God's fairness and goodness or what He has said. It fills us with bitterness, not with thanksgiving.

I have a home that God has provided for me. I've turned off the real estate alerts because God has told me not to covet.

You must not covet your neighbor's house.
EXODUS 20:17 NLT

119

RSVP

Evites are fun—they arrive via email or texts, they're usually beautiful, and they promise a good time. They're easy to deliver and respond to. Most times, they ask, "Will you join us? RSVP and let us know if we can count you in."

Even better are mailed requests. I love receiving fancy embossed invitations, especially to weddings. The paper is elegant and top quality, in keeping with the occasion's significance. Response cards are usually pre-stamped to make replying easy. I have a special cabinet in my kitchen in which I store invitations and greeting cards. Sometimes I thumb through them, grateful for the places and events I've been invited to. I'm careful not to stuff them into the drawer, though, before responding. I might forget, hurting the inviter or overlooking the event altogether.

Likewise, a life of faith is one of constant invitations. God asked Abraham to trust Him when He told Abraham to go to an unknown land. Moses and the Israelites were invited to the Promised Land; Joshua was challenged to lead them. Matthew, Peter, and Andrew were all invited by the Lord to follow Him on a grand adventure, to lay aside their day-to-day concerns and fall in step with Him.

When the Lord invites you to join Him in a new venture filled with promise and possibilities, do you run? Do you stuff the invitation in a drawer without responding, or are you quick to RSVP? I want to be counted on to answer quickly as in Isaiah 6:8, *Yes, I'll come along. Count me in!*

A large crowd came to [Jesus], and he began to teach them. As he walked along, he saw Levi son of Alphaeus sitting at the tax collector's booth. "Follow me," Jesus told him, and Levi got up and followed him.
MARK 2:13–14

Displaced

Although most of us have someplace we call home, we are people on the move. The world is becoming a global village: borders are porous, and airplanes can fly us almost anywhere in a day. It used to take months to circumnavigate the globe; now, we can circle it in about fifty hours. Of course, we can get from here to there quickly, but sometimes that seems to make the world even lonelier.

In some way, we are all displaced people. As Christians, we know we're displaced from our true home in heaven, awaiting us after death. Many of us live in the country or city where we were born, but perhaps our parents or grandparents were immigrants. Or maybe our children will be! So we move across the world, the country, the state, the city. It's a kind of footloose lifestyle now, where we're unsure if the place we call home today will be the same next month or next year.

Sometimes, because of economic instability, people move due to housing costs, new jobs, foreclosed homes, and better opportunities. Some people are displaced emotionally from their families. Many people have no church. Some have no neighbors. Lots have few friends.

Believers have a home—a permanent home, something most of us crave—with Christ (John 14:1–3). Perhaps we might reach out a hand to those who feel adrift and offer them hope for that kind of belonging here on earth, too. Who can you invite into the warmth of your friendship, family, church, life, and faith?

We all remember a time when we were lost, lonely, or frightened, and someone held out a hand to say, *Mi casa es tu casa.*

Jesus says that, for sure.

We are citizens of heaven,
where the Lord Jesus Christ lives.
PHILIPPIANS 3:20 NLT

Bring Home the Bacon

My daughter is a devoted vegetarian due to her great love of animals. Her first word was *dog*. She'd wanted to become a vegetarian since about the age of eight, and finally, when she was twelve, I agreed. I'd found her standing over a roasted chicken, crying, "It has a rib cage."

However, before she gave up meat, she loved bacon: bacon and eggs, BLT sandwiches, bacon sprinkled on pizza. One day when she was young, we were studying Scripture with our kids (Genesis 4:4) and came across the section that called for worshippers to offer the fat portion of the meat as an esteemed offering to the Lord.

I saw her kids' Bible on the coffee table the following day. When I went closer, I could see something wedged inside, a most unusual bookmark. My daughter had gone into the kitchen, pulled a piece of bacon from the refrigerator, and then closed her Bible around it.

"Why did you do that?" I asked.

"I wanted to give God what made Him feel most special," she said. "To let Him know I love Him."

My heart was so touched. When was the last time I had read something in the Bible and taken immediate action to please the Lord? I'm sorry to say at that moment, I could not remember, but I vowed then to follow her lead. I don't know if God loves bacon, but He does tell us a few things we can do to honor Him. To love Him with all our hearts, souls, and strength and love our neighbors as ourselves (Luke 10:27). To act justly, love mercy, and walk humbly with Him (Micah 6:8). And to bring home the bacon—offering our faith—which pleases Him (Hebrews 11:6).

Truly I tell you, unless you change and
become like little children, you will never
enter the kingdom of heaven.
MATTHEW 18:3

DAY 89
Asking for the Recipe

When I was a teenager, we lived next door to a woman who made the most delicious cheesecake you could ever imagine. She was a New Yorker, and there's a reason there is no Minnesota-style cheesecake or New Mexico–style cheesecake, but there is a New York–style cheesecake. It was food fit for a king—or hungry neighbors, in our case.

We wanted to make that cheesecake ourselves, so we asked her for the recipe. Imagine our surprise when she declined to share it. A family secret, she said. But she offered to make us a cheesecake anytime we wanted one. What a deal!

That was my first experience with someone unwilling to share a secret recipe, but it was certainly not the last time I'd heard someone ask for one. If you browse recipes online, you will find many comments such as "I took these to work, and not only were they all eaten, but everyone wanted the recipe." It's satisfying to offer something that people devour, admire, and want to repeat. One friend has been asked so many times for the recipe of one of her dishes that she's saved it to her phone and shares it with anyone who asks whenever she serves the dish.

Wouldn't it be lovely if we could share our faith with as much pride and flourish as we do a treasured recipe? Wouldn't it be thrilling if, after an encounter in which we share or display our faith, a friend or stranger asks us for the "recipe" for facing difficulties, or for our joy, or for life? It's already available in print or digital, you know. Easy to share!

Make the most of every opportunity.
Let your conversation be always full of
grace, seasoned with salt, so that you
may know how to answer everyone.
COLOSSIANS 4:5-6

Pass It On

I love it when I move into a house and find an orderly garden that has been tended and loved. One place offered a wonderful surprise. We had moved in during the autumn, and in the spring, we were delighted to see lovely blossoms gracing the lawn with their flowery presence, drawing the eye and soothing the soul. I offered a silent prayer of thanks for the previous homeowner who had "paid it forward" in the garden for me. I vowed to do likewise.

Many of the homes we have lived in have been rented, and people would often ask, "Why are you spending money on that yard when it isn't yours?"

"But it *is* ours," we'd reply, "for now." And later, it would belong to someone else who would surely appreciate the daffodils in the spring or enjoy harvesting the berries from the bushes in the back. I usually didn't know who would move into our homes after us, but—just as I did with the bulb planter—I felt connected to them through the land and the fruit of our mutual labor.

Kingdom work often involves planting good things into the life of someone you will know only for a short season. You may never see those seeds sprout, but you faithfully planted them, knowing God would cause them to grow. Perhaps you've had the pleasure of accompanying someone on the final leg of the journey to Christ, harvesting what others had planted, watered, and weeded. We are sometimes planters, often weeders, and occasionally harvesters. It's a pleasure to share the garden with our brothers and sisters and to rejoice in the fruit of our mutual labor, knowing that the Master Gardener plots it all.

> *It's not important who does the planting, or who does the watering. What's important is that God makes the seed grow.*
>
> **1 CORINTHIANS 3:7** NLT

Photo Credits